D0509590

DELICIOUSLY HEALTHY VEGETABLES

BY SHAILY LIPA

Copyright© 2012 by Leisure Arts, Inc., 5701 Ranch Drive, Little Rock, Arkansas 72223-9633. 501-868-8800.
www.leisurearts.com. All rights reserved.

This publication is protected under federal copyright laws. Reproduction or distribution of this publication or
any other Leisure Arts publication, including publications which are out of print, is prohibited unless specifically
authorized. This includes, but is not limited to, any form of reproduction or distribution on or through the
Internet, including posting, scanning, or e-mail transmission. We have made every effort to ensure that these
instructions are accurate and complete. We cannot, however, be responsible for human error, typographical
mistakes, or variations in individual work

President and Chief Executive Officer: Rick Barton
Vice President of Editorial: Susan White Sullivan
Vice President of Sales: Mike Behar
Vice President of Operations: Jim Dittrich
Vice President of Finance: Laticia Mull Dittrich
Vice President of Purchasing: Fred F. Pruss
National Sales Director: Martha Adams
Creative Services: Chaska Lucas
Information Technology Director: Hermine Linz
Controller: Francis Caple
Retail Customer Service Manager: Stan Raynor
Director of Designer Relations: Cheryl Johnson
Special Projects Director: Susan Frantz Wiles
Art Publications Director: Rhonda Shelby
Director of eCommerce-Prepress Services: Mark Hawkins

Produced for Leisure Arts, Inc. by Penn Publishing Ltd.
www.penn.co.il
Editor-in-Chief: Rachel Penn
Editor: Rachel Wagner
Design and layout: Michal & Dekel
Photography: Danya Weiner
Styling: Dalit Russo

PRINTED IN CHINA
ISBN-13: 978-1-60900-404-0
Library of Congress Control Number: 2011932594

Cover photography by Danya Weiner

DELICIOUSLY HEALTHY VEGETABLES

BY
SHAILY LIPA

TABLE OF CONTENTS

ABOUT THE AUTHOR

Shaily Lipa is an accomplished recipe writer and cookbook editor who has published five bestselling cookbooks. She began her culinary career as a food journalist for Israel's leading food magazine. Shaily develops recipes for food companies and has been featured on various culinary television shows.

INTRODUCTION

I was raised in a home with a magnificent vegetable heritage. My parents served a fresh vegetable salad with every meal, each one a little different than the day before. They regularly included an array of vegetables in soups, in stews or surrounding the chicken or brisket roasting in the oven. When I ate dinner over at friends' houses, I was surprised to discover that not every kitchen was so veggie-conscious.

The frantic pace and demanding schedules of our modern lives don't allow a lot of time for home cooking. And so vegetables, like other important nutrient groups, are pushed aside in favor of industrial, quick-to-prepare foods.

To my delight, a lot of awareness has been raised about healthy foods in the last decade or so and home cooking is making a comeback. And vegetables, because of their high nutrient content, are enjoying this revival and taking center stage.

In this book, vegetables — raw, blanched, boiled, stir-fried or baked — appear in fragrant pastry, like focaccia teeming with two types of mushrooms, in ribollita soup rich in root vegetables and spinach, in a chicken salad filled with cabbage and peas, and on a skewer of grilled sirloin with peppers and onions. The recipes in all 6 chapters (Starters & Salads, Savory Pastries, Soups, Side Dishes, Pasta & Grains and Meat & Fish) are easy to prepare and make use of readily available ingredients.

I recommend always buying fresh vegetables in small quantities, rather than equipping oneself for a week and a half, thus preventing spoilage and unnecessary waste. It is also best to buy vegetables in season; they will always be fresher, tastier and cheaper than those that have been in cold storage or transported over long distances. Once you know what's fresh and seasonal, choose the recipe you'd like to prepare.

Happy Cooking, Shaily Lipa

VEGETABLE NUTRITION TIPS

Vegetables are full of water, vitamins, minerals, dietary fiber and antioxidants. Vegetables also contain a variety of phytonutrients that appear to help promote health and reduce risk for cancer, heart disease and other conditions. Phytonutrients are the compounds that give plants their bright colors such as red lycopene in tomatoes. The Dietary Guidelines for Americans recommend increasing vegetable intake (to at least 2 $\frac{1}{2}$ cups per day for most people) and eating a variety of vegetables, especially dark green, red and orange vegetables.

Avocado — Contains folate, vitamin E, vitamin K and fiber. Also high in monounsaturated fats which helps lower blood cholesterol if used in place of saturated fats.

Broccoli — High in vitamin C and vitamin K, and a good source of folate, potassium and soluble fiber. Also a source of anti-cancer phytonutrients.

Cabbage — High in vitamin C and vitamin K.

Carrots — High in vitamin A and a good source of soluble fiber.

Mushrooms — High in niacin, pantothenic acid and selenium, and a good source of riboflavin and potassium.

Green Peas — A good source of fiber, vitamin A and vitamin C. Also contain iron and zinc.

Bell Peppers — High in vitamin C. Different colored bell peppers provide different types of phytonutrients making them a nutritious addition to any recipe.

Spinach — High in vitamin A, vitamin K, iron, folate, potassium and magnesium, and a good source of vitamin C.

Sweet Potatoes — High in vitamin A, vitamin C and potassium, and a good source of soluble fiber.

Tomatoes — High in vitamin C and a good source of vitamin A and potassium. Also contain the phytonutrient lycopene which may reduce the risk of prostate and other cancers, and becomes more concentrated during cooking.

STARTERS & SALADS

SPINACH BRUSCHETTA WITH POACHED EGG

SERVES 4

A full breakfast in a single dish! It's important to use very fresh and cold eggs, straight out of the refrigerator.

INGREDIENTS

4 slices Italian bread, sliced about
 $1/2$-inch thick
1 tablespoon olive oil
1 garlic clove, sliced in half

For the eggs:
12 cups water
3 tablespoons white vinegar
 (or apple cider vinegar
 or white wine vinegar)
$1/2$ teaspoon salt
4 eggs, fresh and cold

For the spinach:
1 tablespoon olive oil
10 oz. fresh spinach leaves
Salt and ground black pepper, to taste

PREPARATION

1. Prepare the toasted bread: Brush the slices of bread with a small amount of olive oil. Heat a grill pan over high heat, place bread on pan, olive oil side down, and toast for 2-3 minutes on each side, until grill marks are visible. Rub garlic against the olive oil side of the toasted bread.

2. Prepare the eggs: In a saucepan, bring water, vinegar and salt to a boil. Reduce heat, maintaining water at boiling point. Break 1 egg into a dish. Swirl the boiling water with a wooden spoon creating a whirlpool in the center of the saucepan. Stop swirling and immediately, but carefully, slide the egg into the boiling water. Cook for 3 minutes, until the white congeals and a thin layer envelops the yolk. Remove with a slotted spoon and place on a piece of paper towel. Repeat with 3 remaining eggs.

3. Prepare the spinach: Heat a large pan over medium heat. Add olive oil, spinach, salt and pepper and cook for 2-3 minutes, stirring occasionally, until the spinach softens slightly (the spinach also continues wilting after the heat is turned off). Remove from heat, taste and adjust seasoning with salt and pepper.

4. Serve: Place a mound of cooked spinach on a slice of toast, top with a poached egg and serve immediately.

¤ *Spinach Bruschetta with Poached Egg*

TOMATO, MOZZARELLA & BASIL BRUSCHETTA

SERVES 4

A classic and easy-to-prepare starter. Mozzarella can be substituted with 2 ounces of goat cheese, cut into small cubes.

INGREDIENTS

4 slices Italian bread, sliced about $1/2$-inch thick
1 tablespoon olive oil
1 garlic clove, sliced in half

For the topping:
10 cherry tomatoes, cut into quarters
10 pieces of baby mozzarella cheese, sliced in half
4 basil leaves, thinly sliced
1 tablespoon olive oil
Salt and ground black pepper, to taste

PREPARATION

1. Prepare the toasted bread: Brush the slices of bread with a small amount of olive oil. Heat a grill pan over high heat, place the bread on the pan, olive oil side down, and toast for 2-3 minutes on each side, until grill marks are visible. Rub garlic on the olive oil side of the toasted bread.

2. Prepare the topping: Mix tomatoes, mozzarella, basil, olive oil and a small amount of salt and pepper in a bowl.

3. Serve: Place a mound of the topping on a slice of toast and serve immediately.

PEA & FETA CHEESE BRUSCHETTA

SERVES 4

A spring bruschetta with garden-fresh peas — one of the greenest and tastiest of the healthy superstars!

INGREDIENTS

4 slices Italian bread, sliced about $1/2$-inch thick
1 tablespoon olive oil
1 garlic clove, sliced in half

For the topping:
$1^1/_2$ cups shelled fresh green peas
2 tablespoons olive oil
Zest of $1/_4$ lemon, finely grated
1 tablespoon lemon juice
Salt and ground black pepper, to taste
3 oz. feta cheese, crumbled

PREPARATION

1. Prepare the toasted bread: Brush the slices of bread with a small amount of olive oil. Heat a grill pan over high heat, place the bread on the pan, olive oil side down, and toast for 2-3 minutes on each side, until grill marks are visible. Rub garlic on the olive oil side of the toasted bread.

2. Prepare the topping: Cook peas for 3-4 minutes in salted boiling water, until soft. Drain well and transfer to a bowl. Coarsely mash the peas with a fork. Add olive oil, lemon zest, lemon juice, salt and pepper and stir.

3. Serve: Place a mound of the pea topping on a slice of toast, sprinkle with feta cheese and serve immediately.

MUSHROOM QUESADILLAS

SERVES 2

An alternative to typical Mexican grilled cheese — this version has sautéed mushrooms and mozzarella cheese.

INGREDIENTS

For the filling:
2 tablespoons olive oil
2 shallots, finely chopped
8 oz. button or cremini mushrooms, cut into 1/4-inch slices
1/2–1 red chili pepper, thinly sliced (optional)
Salt and ground black pepper, to taste
1 cup mozzarella cheese, shredded
2 tablespoons cilantro, finely chopped

For the tortillas:
Olive oil, to grease the pan
4 tortillas (whole-wheat is preferable)

PREPARATION

1. Prepare the filling: Heat a large pan over medium heat, add olive oil and shallots and cook for 2-3 minutes, stirring occasionally, until shallots are tender. Add mushrooms, chili, salt and pepper and sauté for 2 minutes, until mushrooms are tender. Taste and adjust seasoning with salt and pepper. Transfer to a bowl with a slotted spoon, discarding liquid. Cool for 15 minutes. Add mozzarella and cilantro.

2. Prepare the quesadilla: Place half the amount of filling on one tortilla and cover with another tortilla. Heat a nonstick pan over medium heat and grease with a small amount of olive oil. Place the quesadilla in the pan and sauté for 2-3 minutes, until the bottom tortilla turns golden brown. Carefully flip over and fry on the other side until the second tortilla turns golden brown and the cheese melts. Repeat process with second quesadilla.

3. Serve: Cut into triangles and serve immediately.

¤ *Bottom: Corn & Pepper Quesadillas (p. 18) / Top: Mushroom Quesadillas*

CORN & PEPPER QUESADILLAS

SERVES 2

¤ *see photo on p.17*

An especially colorful and tasty quesadilla. Add a side salad and you've got a complete, wholesome meal.

INGREDIENTS

For the filling:
1 cup mozzarella cheese, shredded
$1/3$ cup corn kernels
$1/2$ medium red pepper, cut in $1/4$-inch cubes
1 green onion, thinly sliced (white and green parts)
2 tablespoons cilantro, finely chopped
1 teaspoon hot sauce (optional)
Salt and ground black pepper, to taste

For the tortillas:
Olive oil, to grease the pan
4 tortillas (whole-wheat is preferable)

PREPARATION

1. Prepare the filling: Mix the ingredients for the filling in a bowl. Taste and adjust seasoning with salt and pepper.

2. Prepare the quesadilla: Place half the amount of filling on one tortilla and cover with another tortilla. Heat a nonstick pan over medium heat and grease with a small amount of olive oil. Place the quesadilla in the pan and fry for 2-3 minutes, until the bottom tortilla turns golden brown. Carefully flip over and fry on the other side until the second tortilla turns golden brown and the cheese melts. Repeat process with second quesadilla.

3. Serve: Cut into triangles and serve immediately.

GUACAMOLE

SERVES 4-6

An avocado salad of Mexican origin that has become an international household staple when it comes to dips.

INGREDIENTS

3 medium Mexican (Hass) avocados, peeled and cut into $1/2$-inch cubes
1 small red onion, peeled and finely chopped
1 medium tomato, seeded and cut into $1/4$-inch cubes
$1/3$ cup cilantro, finely chopped
$1/2$–1 teaspoon hot sauce
1 teaspoon smooth Dijon mustard
$1/4$ cup lemon juice
Salt and ground black pepper, to taste

PREPARATION

Mix all ingredients in a bowl, taste and adjust seasoning with salt and pepper. Add additional lemon juice, as needed.

✱ The guacamole can be stored in the refrigerator with plastic wrap pressed directly onto the surface of the dip for up to 2 days.

¤ *Cucumber & Beet Tzatziki*

CUCUMBER & BEET TZATZIKI

SERVES 6

Beets are added to classic tzatziki, bestowing it with a gorgeous deep purple color and wondrous earthy flavor.

INGREDIENTS

2 cups plain Greek-style
    yogurt
1 medium beet, cooked,
    peeled & coarsely grated
1 medium cucumber,
    coarsely grated and
    pressed to release liquid
2 garlic cloves, crushed
2 tablespoons mint,
    finely chopped
Salt and ground black
    pepper, to taste

PREPARATION

Mix all the ingredients in a bowl. Taste and adjust seasoning with salt and pepper. Serve immediately on toasted or fresh bread.

* The tzatziki can be stored in an airtight container in refrigerator for up to 2 days, but it will release some liquid. Simply pour out the excess liquid prior to serving.

SPINACH TZATZIKI

SERVES 6

Spinach, rather than traditional cucumber, gives this Greek dip an added green vegetable 'oomph'.

INGREDIENTS

1 tablespoon olive oil
8 oz. spinach leaves
2 cups plain Greek-style
    yogurt
1 tablespoon lemon juice
1 tablespoon olive oil
2 garlic cloves, crushed
Salt and ground black
    pepper, to taste

PREPARATION

Heat a large pan over medium heat. Add olive oil and spinach and cook for 2-3 minutes, stirring occasionally, until the spinach softens slightly. (The spinach also continues wilting after the heat is turned off.) Remove from heat and transfer to a strainer. Cool completely. Wring out the cooked spinach by hand. Chop coarsely and transfer to a bowl. Add the yogurt, lemon juice, olive oil, garlic, salt and pepper and stir. Taste and adjust seasoning with salt and pepper. Serve immediately on toasted or fresh bread.

* The tzatziki can be stored in an airtight container in refrigerator for up to 2 days, but it will release some liquid. Simply pour out the excess liquid prior to serving.

¤ *Pea Pancakes*

PEA PANCAKES

MAKES 15 SMALL PANCAKES

*A light and healthy alternative
to traditional potato pancakes.
Serve with thick yogurt for
a real treat.*

INGREDIENTS

3 cups shelled fresh green peas
1/4 cup mint, finely chopped
1/4 cup breadcrumbs
1/4 cup Parmesan cheese, finely grated
2 tablespoons plain Greek-style
    yogurt
1 shallot, finely chopped
2 large eggs

For frying:
Canola oil

For serving:
Plain Greek-style yogurt

PREPARATION

1. Cook peas for 3-4 minutes in salted boiling water, until soft. Transfer to strainer and cool for about 5 minutes until just warm.

2. Transfer the peas to a food processor, add remaining ingredients and blend into a smooth, uniform mixture.

3. Fill a medium nonstick frying pan with a 1/4-inch of canola oil and heat over medium heat. Fry a single small pancake to test the seasoning, taste and adjust seasoning of the mixture with salt and pepper.

4. Ladle 1 heaping tablespoon of batter per pancake into the pan. Fry for 3-4 minutes, until golden. Flip over and fry for 2 minutes on the other side. Transfer to a paper towel to remove excess oil. Repeat the process with remaining batter.

5. Serve pancakes with a dollop of thick yogurt (optional).

✳ The pancakes can be stored in an airtight container in refrigerator for up to 3 days. Reheating is recommended prior to serving.

ZUCCHINI
&
RICOTTA
FRITTERS

MAKES 12
SMALL FRITTERS

Ricotta cheese makes these fritters especially soft and creamy. Serve with Cucumber & Beet Tzatziki — see page 21. If you prefer a basic tzatziki, substitute the beet with an additional cucumber.

INGREDIENTS

2 medium zucchini, shredded and pressed to release liquid
$^3/_4$ cup ricotta cheese
1 large egg
$^1/_3$ cup breadcrumbs
$^1/_4$ cup chives, finely chopped
2 garlic cloves, crushed
Salt and ground black pepper, to taste

For frying:
Canola oil

PREPARATION

1. Mix all the ingredients in a bowl to form a uniform mixture.

2. Fill a medium nonstick frying pan with $^1/_4$-inch of canola oil and heat over medium heat. Fry a single small fritter to test the seasoning, taste and adjust seasoning of the mixture with salt and pepper.

3. Ladle 1 heaping tablespoon of batter per fritter into the pan. Fry for 3-4 minutes, until golden. Flip over and fry for 2 minutes on the other side. Transfer to a paper towel to remove excess oil. Repeat the process with remaining batter.

✳ The fritters can be stored in an airtight container in refrigerator for up to 3 days. Reheating is recommended prior to serving.

MEDITERRANEAN FRITTATA

SERVES 4-6

A colorful and tasty frittata checkered with cherry tomatoes, Greek olives, feta cheese and strips of basil.

INGREDIENTS

2 tablespoons olive oil
2 shallots, coarsely chopped
6 eggs
Salt and ground black pepper, to taste
8 cherry tomatoes, sliced in half
6 Kalamata olives, pitted and halved
3 oz. feta cheese, crumbled
6 basil leaves, thinly sliced

PREPARATION

1. Preheat oven to 350°F.

2. Heat a medium-sized, oven-safe pan (pan will be transferred to oven for cooking) over medium heat. Add olive oil and shallots and sauté for 2-3 minutes, stirring occasionally, until the shallots are tender. Distribute the shallots evenly around the pan.

3. Beat the eggs, salt and pepper in a bowl and pour into the pan. Arrange the halved cherry tomatoes and olives in the frittata and sprinkle with feta and basil. Cook for 3 minutes, until the edges of the frittata start to solidify.

4. Transfer the pan to the oven and bake for 15 minutes, until lightly golden.

✱ The frittata can be stored in an airtight container in refrigerator for up to 2 days. Reheating is recommended prior to serving.

GREEN FRITTATA

SERVES 4-6

A frittata is an Italian omelet that rises in the oven. This green version is chock full of broccoli, peas and spinach.

INGREDIENTS

1 cup small broccoli florets
1 cup shelled fresh green peas
2 tablespoons olive oil
2 shallots, coarsely chopped
3 oz. spinach leaves, coarsely chopped
6 large eggs
Salt and ground black pepper, to taste

PREPARATION

1. Preheat oven to 350°F.

2. Cook broccoli and peas for 3-4 minutes in salted boiling water, until tender. Transfer to strainer.

3. Heat a medium-sized, oven-safe pan (pan will be transferred to oven for cooking) over medium heat. Add olive oil and shallots and sauté for 2-3 minutes, stirring occasionally, until shallots are tender. Add broccoli, peas and spinach, scattering them evenly throughout the pan.

4. Beat the eggs, salt and pepper in a bowl and pour into the pan. Cook for 3 minutes, until the edges of the frittata start to come together.

5. Transfer the pan to the oven and bake for 15 minutes, until lightly golden.

✱ The frittata can be stored in an airtight container in refrigerator for up to 2 days. Reheating is recommended prior to serving.

¤ *Green Frittata*

PERFECT GREEN SALAD

SERVES 6

The perfect green salad is one that features the holy trinity of very fresh lettuce, sweet fruit and crisp nuts.

INGREDIENTS

2 heads of lettuce (two varieties are preferable), removed from stem, washed and well dried

Seasonal fruit (1 mango or 2 nectarines or 12 strawberries or 2 persimmons), cut into 3/4-inch cubes

3/4 cup nuts (any variety you like)

For the dressing:
1/3 cup olive oil
2 tablespoons lemon juice
2 tablespoons apple cider vinegar
1 teaspoon mustard
1 teaspoon honey
Salt and ground black pepper, to taste

PREPARATION

1. Tear lettuce into bite-sized pieces, place in a bowl and sprinkle with cubes of fruit and nuts.

2. In a separate container, mix dressing ingredients well, pour over salad and toss. Serve immediately.

PANZANELLA SALAD

SERVES 4-6

INGREDIENTS

5 medium tomatoes, cut into
   1-inch cubes
3 medium peppers (red or yellow),
   cut into 1-inch cubes
1 small red onion, cut in half and
   thinly sliced
12 Kalamata olives, pitted
Day-old ciabatta, broken into pieces

For the dressing:
$1/3$ cup olive oil
2 tablespoons lemon juice
2 tablespoons red wine vinegar
1 garlic clove, crushed
$1/4$ teaspoon sugar
Salt and ground black pepper, to taste

For serving:
12 oregano leaves or small basil leaves

It's best to use day-old ciabatta or other Italian bread, because dry bread will better absorb the dressing.

PREPARATION

1. Mix the tomatoes, peppers, onion, olives and ciabatta pieces in a bowl.

2. Mix the dressing ingredients well, add to salad and stir.

3. Sprinkle with the oregano or basil leaves and serve. You can also wait 30 minutes for the bread to soften before serving.

ZUCCHINI, YOGURT & MINT SALAD

SERVES 4-6

Zucchini and mint make the perfect pair. This salad features a double dose of mint — fresh and dried.

INGREDIENTS

4 medium zucchini, sliced in half lengthwise
2 tablespoons olive oil
1 small red onion, cut in half and thinly sliced
2 tablespoons fresh mint, finely chopped

For the dressing:
1 cup plain Greek-style yogurt
1 tablespoon lemon juice
$1/2$ teaspoon dried mint
Salt and ground black pepper, to taste

PREPARATION

1. Slice the zucchini into $1/4$-inch thick half-moons. Heat a large pan over medium heat, add olive oil and zucchini, and sauté for 10 minutes, until zucchini is golden brown on both sides. (Sautéing in two batches is recommended.) Transfer to a bowl and cool for 10 minutes. Add onion and mint.

2. Mix dressing ingredients well, add to salad and stir. Taste and adjust seasoning with salt and pepper.

RED LENTIL, CARROT & WALNUT SALAD

SERVES 6

In addition to being super-healthy, red lentils cook quickly (in just a few minutes), taste great served cold and fill you up.

INGREDIENTS

2 cups red lentils, rinsed and drained
2 medium carrots, peeled and coarsely grated
1 cup toasted walnuts, coarsely chopped
$1/2$ cup cilantro, coarsely chopped

For the dressing:
$1/3$ cup olive oil
$1/4$ cup lemon juice
2 tablespoons orange juice
$1 1/2$ teaspoons honey
Salt and ground black pepper, to taste

PREPARATION

1. Place the lentils in a saucepan, cover with water (4 inches above the lentils) and cook for 5-10 minutes, until they begin to soften but before they start losing their shape. (Pay attention because this happens quickly!) Drain well. Transfer to a bowl and cool for 10 minutes. Add grated carrot, walnuts and cilantro.

2. Mix dressing ingredients well, add to salad and stir. Taste and adjust seasoning with salt and pepper.

✳ The salad can be stored in an airtight container in refrigerator for up to 2 days.

POTATO, RED ONION, SPROUT & ROQUEFORT SALAD

SERVES 4

Instead of a heavy cream dressing, this salad has a light and healthy one that complements the potato's natural flavor without overwhelming it.

INGREDIENTS

5 medium potatoes, peeled and cut into 1 1/2-inch cubes
1 tablespoon salt
1 small red onion, cut in half and thinly sliced
1 cup sunflower sprouts
1/4 cup parsley, finely chopped
3 oz. Roquefort cheese, coarsely crumbled

For the dressing:
1/4 cup canola oil
2 tablespoons white wine vinegar
1 teaspoon coarse grain Dijon mustard
1 level teaspoon sugar
Salt and ground black pepper, to taste

PREPARATION

1. Place the potato cubes in a saucepan, cover with water (1 inch above the potatoes), add salt and bring to a boil. Reduce heat and cook for 15 minutes, until the potatoes are tender but still solid. Drain well, transfer to a bowl and cool for 10 minutes. Add onion, sprouts and parsley.

2. Mix dressing ingredients until the sugar is dissolved. Add to the salad and stir. Top with Roquefort cheese and serve immediately.

✳ The salad can be stored in an airtight container in refrigerator for up to 2 days.

¤ *Potato, Red Onion, Sprout & Roquefort Salad*

WARM COLESLAW SALAD

SERVES 4

Classic coleslaw gets a twist with some stir-frying.

INGREDIENTS

2 tablespoons olive oil
1 medium onion, finely chopped
$1/2$ medium cabbage, cut into thin strips
2 medium carrots, peeled and julienned
$1/4$ cup parsley, finely chopped

For the dressing:
2 tablespoons olive oil
2 tablespoons apple cider vinegar
1 teaspoon honey
1 teaspoon sugar
Salt and ground black pepper, to taste

PREPARATION

1. Heat a large nonstick pan over medium heat, add olive oil and onion and sauté for 5 minutes, stirring occasionally, until the onion is soft. Add cabbage and carrot and stir-fry for 3-4 minutes, until the vegetables start to soften. Transfer to a bowl and add parsley.

2. Mix the dressing ingredients well, pour over salad and stir. Taste and adjust seasoning with salt and pepper.

✱ The salad can be stored in an airtight container in refrigerator for up to 2 days.

PURPLE CABBAGE, APPLE & PECAN SALAD

SERVES 6-8

This salad stands the test of time and can be made in advance for picnics and brunches, though it will lose some of its initial crispness.

INGREDIENTS

1 medium purple cabbage, cut into thin strips
1 medium green apple, cut in half and thinly sliced
1 red apple, cut in half and thinly sliced
1 cup pecans (or walnuts), coarsely chopped

For the dressing:
$1/4$ cup canola oil
2 tablespoons apple cider vinegar
2 tablespoons lemon juice
1 garlic clove, crushed
1 teaspoon smooth Dijon mustard
1 teaspoon sugar
Salt and ground black pepper, to taste

PREPARATION

1. Place the cabbage strips and apple slices in a large bowl.

2. Mix the dressing ingredients until the sugar dissolves, pour over salad and stir. Sprinkle with nuts and serve.

✱ The salad can be stored in an airtight container in refrigerator for up to 2 days.

¤ *Purple Cabbage, Apple & Pecan Salad*

DICED VEGETABLE SALAD WITH SAVORY GRANOLA

SERVES 6

This diced vegetable salad features a surprise topping of savory granola with a hint of za'atar. The savory crisp granola also goes well with yogurt.

INGREDIENTS

For 2 cups savory granola:
1 tablespoon olive oil
1 cup old-fashioned oats
$^1/_4$ cup slivered almonds
$^1/_4$ cup sunflower seeds
$^1/_4$ cup pumpkin seeds
2 tablespoons sesame seeds
1 tablespoon dried za'atar
   (if unavailable, substitute with Herbes de Provence)
$^1/_2$ teaspoon salt

For the salad:
4 medium tomatoes, finely diced
4 medium cucumbers, finely diced
2 medium peppers (yellow or orange), finely diced
1 medium red onion, finely diced
$^1/_3$ cup parsley, finely chopped
$^1/_3$ cup mint, finely chopped

For the dressing:
4 tablespoons olive oil
3 tablespoons lemon juice
Salt and ground black pepper, to taste

PREPARATION

1. Prepare the granola: Heat a large nonstick pan over medium-low heat. Add olive oil and oats and stir for about a minute, until the oats absorb the oil. Add the remaining granola ingredients and sauté over medium heat for 3-4 minutes, stirring continuously, until golden.

2. Prepare the salad: Mix all the salad and dressing ingredients together in a bowl, taste and adjust seasoning with salt and pepper.

3. Serve: Sprinkle with savory granola (about half the quantity prepared) and serve immediately.

✶ Remaining granola can be stored in an airtight container in pantry for up to 2 weeks and served with another salad or eaten for breakfast with yogurt.

¤ *Diced Vegetable Salad with Savory Granola*

FENNEL & PISTACHIO SALAD

SERVES 4-6

The fennel's anise flavor is an excellent complement to the pistachio's sweetness.

INGREDIENTS

4 medium fennel bulbs, leaves removed and cut into $1/4$-inch thick slices
2 tablespoons olive oil
2 tablespoons lemon juice
1 teaspoon apple cider vinegar
Salt and ground black pepper, to taste

For serving:
$1/4$ cup pistachios, shelled and lightly toasted

PREPARATION

Mix fennel, olive oil, lemon juice, vinegar, salt and pepper in a bowl. Taste and adjust seasoning with salt and pepper. Sprinkle with pistachios and serve.

* The salad can be stored in an airtight container in refrigerator for up to 2 days.

GREEN BEAN & DRIED CRANBERRY SALAD

SERVES 6

This salad of fresh green beans is dotted with dried cranberries and sesame seeds. Cranberries can also be substituted with the same quantity of fresh pomegranate seeds, when in season.

INGREDIENTS

2 pounds fresh green beans
1 cup dried cranberries
2 tablespoons sesame seeds, toasted

For the dressing:
$1/4$ cup canola oil
2 tablespoons white wine vinegar
1 garlic clove, crushed
1 teaspoon smooth Dijon mustard
1 teaspoon honey
Salt and ground black pepper, to taste

PREPARATION

1. Cook green beans for 3-4 minutes in salted boiling water, until they soften but are still crisp. Drain well, transfer to a bowl and cool for 10 minutes. Add dried cranberries and sesame seeds.

2. Mix all the dressing ingredients well, add to salad and stir. Taste and adjust seasoning with salt and pepper.

✶ The salad can be stored in an airtight container in refrigerator for up to 2 days.

¤ *Green Bean & Dried Cranberry Salad*

SAVORY
PASTRIES

ASPARAGUS, PESTO & RICOTTA TARTS

MAKES 12 INDIVIDUAL TARTS

For best results, choose a puff pastry made from real butter, rather than from margarine.

INGREDIENTS

For the filling:
9 oz. ricotta cheese
$1/3$ cup pesto
Salt and ground black pepper, to taste

For the tarts:
3 sheets (26 oz.) puff pastry, thawed according to package instructions
1 bunch asparagus, trimmed

For the glazing:
1 egg yolk, beaten with 1 teaspoon milk

PREPARATION

1. Preheat oven to 350°F and line two baking sheets with parchment paper.

2. Prepare the filling: Mix the filling ingredients in a bowl, taste and adjust seasoning with salt and pepper. The filling can be prepared in advance and covered and stored in the refrigerator.

3. Prepare the tarts: Roll pastry into a 10 x 10 inch sheet. Cut out 5 x 5 inch squares of pastry and place them on baking sheets. Gently mark off $1/2$-inch edges using a knife, but without cutting into the pastry. Slice the asparagus into pieces, each 3 inches long. Spread the filling onto the dough, making sure to keep it inside the edges and arrange the asparagus on top. Brush the pastry edges with beaten egg.

4. Bake for 25 minutes, until golden brown.

＊ Tarts can be covered and stored in refrigerator up to 3 days. Reheating is recommended prior to serving.

¤ *Asparagus, Pesto & Ricotta Tarts*

ONION & HERB FLATBREAD

MAKES 2 MEDIUM
FLATBREADS

This bread is sort of a cross between pita and focaccia, with especially flavor-rich dough thanks to the onion and herbs.

INGREDIENTS

2 tablespoons olive oil
1 large onion, cut in half
    and thinly sliced
1¼ teaspoons active dry yeast
1 tablespoon dark brown sugar
¾ cup warm water
1 cup whole-wheat flour
1 cup all-purpose flour

½ teaspoon salt
2 tablespoons rosemary, coarsely
    chopped
2 tablespoons thyme, coarsely
    chopped

For the topping:
Pinch of sea salt

PREPARATION

1. Heat a medium-sized pan over medium heat, add olive oil and onion and sauté for about 5 minutes, until the onion is tender.

2. In the mixing bowl of an electric mixer, dissolve the yeast and sugar in the warm water and let stand for about 10 minutes, or until foamy on top. Add cooked onion and remaining ingredients. Mix with a dough hook at medium-low speed for about 10 minutes, until dough is soft and slightly sticky.

3. Transfer dough to a greased bowl, turning once to coat dough, and cover with plastic wrap. Let rise in a warm place 1 hour or until doubled in size.

4. Preheat the oven to 400°F. Divide dough in half. On a piece of parchment paper, roll each half into a ¼-inch-thick round or oval. Transfer, with parchment paper, to baking sheets and sprinkle with a small amount of sea salt. Cover with a damp towel and allow dough to rise for another 30 minutes.

5. Bake for 15-20 minutes, until golden brown.

✱ Flatbreads can be covered and stored at room temperature for up to 2 days.

MUSHROOM & HERB FOCACCIA

MAKES 2 MEDIUM FOCACCIA BREADS

Feel free to improvise with the variety of mushrooms in this recipe (it's always best to go for the freshest mushrooms available), but using at least two varieties will result in a richer flavor and texture.

INGREDIENTS

For the dough:

2¼ teaspoons active dry yeast

1 tablespoon dark brown sugar

1¼ cups warm water

2 cups all-purpose flour

1½ cups whole-wheat flour

¼ cup olive oil

1½ teaspoons salt

For the topping:

2 tablespoons olive oil

8 oz. button or cremini mushrooms, cut into ¼-inch slices

8 oz. portobello mushrooms, cut into ¼-inch slices

2 tablespoons parsley, coarsely chopped

2 tablespoons basil, coarsely chopped

1 tablespoon rosemary, coarsely chopped

Salt and ground black pepper, to taste

PREPARATION

1. Prepare the dough: In the mixing bowl of an electric mixer, dissolve the yeast and sugar in the warm water and let stand for about 10 minutes, or until foamy on top. Add remaining dough ingredients and mix with a dough hook at medium-low speed for about 10 minutes, until dough is soft and slightly sticky.

2. Transfer dough to a greased bowl, turning once to coat dough, and cover with plastic wrap. Let rise in a warm place 1 hour or until doubled in size.

3. In the meantime, prepare the topping: Heat a large pan over medium heat, add olive oil and mushrooms and sauté for 10 minutes, until the mushrooms are tender and the pan is dry. Remove from heat, add herbs, salt and pepper and stir. Taste and adjust seasoning with salt and pepper.

4. Prepare the focaccia: Divide dough in half. On a piece of parchment paper, roll each half into a ¼-inch-thick round or oval. Transfer, with parchment paper, to baking sheets. Cover with a damp towel and allow dough to rise for another 30 minutes.

5. Preheat the oven to 400°F. With your finger, make depressions in the dough. Place the topping on the dough.

6. Bake for 20-25 minutes, until golden brown.

＊ Focaccia bread can be covered and stored for up to 2 days in refrigerator. Reheating is recommended prior to serving.

FRESH & SUN-DRIED TOMATO FOCACCIA

MAKES 2 MEDIUM FOCACCIA BREADS

Two types of tomatoes make for an especially supple and tasty focaccia; sun-dried tomatoes, packed in olive oil, are incorporated into the dough, while fresh tomatoes adorn the top.

INGREDIENTS

2¼ teaspoons active dry yeast

1 tablespoon dark brown sugar

1¼ cups warm water

2 cups all-purpose flour

1½ cups whole-wheat flour

⅓ cup sun-dried tomatoes, packed in olive oil, thoroughly drained (reserving oil) and sliced into thin strips

¼ cup oil, using reserved oil from sun-dried tomatoes plus olive oil, if needed

1 teaspoon salt

For the topping:

2 tablespoons olive oil

2 medium tomatoes, thinly sliced

1 sprig rosemary, chopped

2 tablespoons sesame seeds

Pinch of sea salt

PREPARATION

1. In the mixing bowl of an electric mixer, dissolve the yeast and sugar in the warm water and let stand for about 10 minutes, or until foamy on top. Add remaining dough ingredients and mix with a dough hook at medium-low speed for about 10 minutes, until dough is soft and slightly sticky.

2. Transfer dough to a greased bowl, turning once to coat dough, and cover with plastic wrap. Let rise in a warm place 1 hour or until doubled in size. Divide dough in half. On a piece of parchment paper, roll each half into a ¼-inch-thick round or oval. Transfer, with parchment paper, to baking sheets. Cover with a damp towel and allow dough to rise for another 30 minutes.

3. Preheat the oven to 400°F. With your finger, make depressions in the dough. Drizzle generously with olive oil, arrange the slices of tomato and sprinkle with rosemary, sesame seeds and sea salt.

4. Bake for 20-25 minutes, until golden brown.

∗ Focaccia bread can be covered and stored for up to 2 days in refrigerator. Reheating is recommended prior to serving.

¤ *Fresh & Sun-Dried Tomato Focaccia*

ZUCCHINI & GOAT CHEESE PIZZA

MAKES 2 MEDIUM PIZZAS
OR 4 SMALL PIZZAS

A sauceless pizza with a superb zucchini and goat cheese topping.

INGREDIENTS

For the dough:
1¼ teaspoons active dry yeast
1 tablespoon dark brown sugar
¾ cup warm water
1 cup whole-wheat flour
1 cup all-purpose flour
2 tablespoons olive oil
1 teaspoon salt

For the topping:
2 medium zucchini, cut into
  ¼-inch thick slices
7 oz. goat cheese, cut into
  ¼-inch thick slices
1 tablespoon fresh thyme

PREPARATION

1. Prepare the dough: In the mixing bowl of an electric mixer, dissolve the yeast and sugar in the warm water and let stand for about 10 minutes or until foamy on top. Add remaining dough ingredients and mix with a dough hook at medium-low speed for about 10 minutes, until dough is soft and slightly sticky.

2. Transfer dough to a greased bowl, turning once to coat dough, and cover with plastic wrap. Let rise in a warm place 1 hour or until doubled in size.

3. Prepare the pizza: Preheat the oven to 400°F. Divide the dough in half and roll out each half on a piece of parchment paper into a 10-inch circle, ¼-inch thick (or divide into 4 pieces and roll out into 5-inch circles). Transfer, with parchment paper, to baking sheets. Arrange the zucchini, goat cheese and thyme on the dough.

4. Bake for 20-25 minutes, until golden brown around the edges.

✱ The pizza can be covered and stored in refrigerator up to 3 days. Reheating is recommended prior to serving.

MEDITERRANEAN PIZZA WITH EGGPLANT, TOMATOES & FETA

MAKES 2 MEDIUM PIZZAS
OR 4 SMALL PIZZAS

INGREDIENTS

For the dough:

1¼ teaspoons active dry yeast
1 tablespoon dark brown sugar
¾ cup warm water
1 cup whole-wheat flour
1 cup all-purpose flour
2 tablespoons olive oil
1 teaspoon salt

For the topping:

30 cherry tomatoes, cut in half (if available, use 2 different colors)
½ medium eggplant, cut into ½-inch cubes
1 small red onion, cut in half and thinly sliced
8 oz. feta cheese, crumbled

Thin pizza crust is topped with halved cherry tomatoes, cubes of eggplant, slices of red onion and crumbled feta cheese — it doesn't get more Mediterranean than this.

PREPARATION

1. Prepare the dough: In the mixing bowl of an electric mixer, dissolve the yeast and sugar in the warm water and let stand for about 10 minutes or until foamy on top. Add remaining dough ingredients and mix with a dough hook at medium-low speed for about 10 minutes, until dough is soft and slightly sticky.

2. Transfer dough to a greased bowl, turning once to coat dough, and cover with plastic wrap. Let rise in a warm place 1 hour or until doubled in size.

3. Prepare the pizza: Preheat the oven to 400°F. Divide the dough in half and roll out each half on a piece of parchment paper into a 10-inch circle, ¼-inch thick (or divide into 4 pieces and roll out into 5-inch circles). Transfer, with parchment paper, to baking sheets. Arrange tomatoes, eggplant cubes and onion slices on the dough and sprinkle with feta cheese.

4. Bake for 20-25 minutes, until golden brown around the edges.

✱ The pizza can be covered and stored in refrigerator up to 3 days. Reheating is recommended prior to serving.

SWEET POTATO & GOAT CHEESE QUICHE

FOR AN 11-INCH
QUICHE PLATE

A lush quiche bursting with goodness: crisp pastry, cubes of golden sweet potato, soft goat cheese and chives that carry a spicy bite.

INGREDIENTS

For the crust:
2 cups all-purpose flour
3/4 cup cold butter, cubed
1 teaspoon salt
1/2 teaspoon sugar
1 egg

For the filling:
2 tablespoons olive oil
1 medium sweet potato, peeled and cut into 1-inch cubes
5 oz. goat cheese, cut into 1-inch cubes
1 cup half and half
3 eggs, beaten
2 tablespoons chives, chopped
Salt and ground black pepper, to taste

PREPARATION

1. Prepare the crust: Combine flour, butter, salt and sugar in a food processor. Process until mixture resembles coarse meal. Add egg and mix until dough forms a ball. On a floured surface, roll out the dough into a 13-inch circle. Line the bottom and sides of the quiche plate with dough and trim away excess. Prick dough with a fork and transfer to the freezer for 30 minutes.

2. Preheat the oven to 350°F. Bake for 15-20 minutes, until lightly golden. Cool for 10 minutes.

3. Prepare the filling: Add olive oil and sweet potato to a large skillet over medium heat and sauté for 7 minutes, until golden brown. Remove from heat and cool for 10 minutes.

4. Increase oven temperature to 375°F. Combine remaining ingredients in a bowl and stir in sweet potatoes. Pour into the crust and bake for 30-35 minutes, until filling is set and is golden brown.

✳ Quiche can be covered and stored in refrigerator up to 3 days. Reheating is recommended prior to serving.

SPINACH & ROASTED PEPPER QUICHE

FOR AN 11-INCH
QUICHE PLATE

*An impressive and stylish
quiche that always wins
compliments.*

INGREDIENTS

For the crust:
2 cups all-purpose flour
³/₄ cup cold butter, cubed
1 teaspoon salt
¹/₂ teaspoon sugar
1 egg

For the filling:
1 tablespoon olive oil
7 oz. fresh spinach leaves
2 red peppers, roasted and cut
   into 1-inch long strips
1 cup mozzarella cheese, shredded
1 cup half and half
3 eggs, beaten
2 garlic cloves, finely chopped
Salt and ground black pepper, to taste

PREPARATION

1. Prepare the crust: Combine flour, butter, salt and sugar in a food processor. Process until mixture resembles coarse meal. Add egg and mix until dough forms a ball. On a floured surface, roll out the dough into a 13-inch circle. Line the bottom and sides of the quiche plate with dough and trim away excess. Prick dough with a fork and transfer to the freezer for 30 minutes.

2. Preheat the oven to 350°F. Bake for 15-20 minutes, until lightly golden. Cool for 10 minutes.

3. Prepare the filling: Add olive oil and spinach to a large skillet over medium heat and sauté for 2-3 minutes, stirring continuously, until the spinach wilts. Remove from heat and transfer to a colander. Cool thoroughly.

4. Increase oven temperature to 375°F. Press any liquid from cooked spinach by hand and chop coarsely. Combine remaining ingredients in a bowl and stir in spinach. Pour into the crust and bake for 30-35 minutes, until filling is set and is golden brown.

✳ Quiche can be covered and stored in refrigerator up to 3 days. Reheating is recommended prior to serving.

¤ *Spinach & Roasted Pepper Quiche*

CARAMELIZED ONION & CHEESE TART

SERVES 8-10

Caramelized onion and cheese is a winning combination. Add a flaky puff pastry base and you've got a tart that's impossible to resist.

INGREDIENTS

For the tart:
1 sheet puff pastry, thawed according to package instructions
5 medium red onions, cut into $1/2$-inch rings
8 oz. mozzarella cheese, shredded
4 oz. goat cheese, cut into $1/2$-inch cubes

For the filling:
3 tablespoons olive oil
$1/3$ cup dry red wine
3 tablespoons balsamic vinegar
3 tablespoons dark brown sugar

For serving:
1 sprig thyme, chopped

PREPARATION

1. Prepare the caramelized onion: Heat a large pan over medium heat, add olive oil, wine, balsamic vinegar and sugar, stir and bring to a boil. Place onion rings in pan and cook for 5 minutes, without turning them, until the liquids reduce. Cool thoroughly.

2. Preheat the oven to 400°F. Line a baking sheet with parchment paper.

3. Prepare the tart: Lay the pastry on parchment paper. Place onions on pastry, caramelized side up, to within $3/4$ inch of edges. Cover with mozzarella and then arrange the goat cheese.

4. Bake for 20-25 minutes, until golden brown. Remove from oven and top with thyme.

* The tart can be covered and stored in refrigerator up to 3 days. Reheating is recommended prior to serving.

TOMATO, ANCHOVY & OLIVE TART

SERVES 8-10

This Mediterranean tart boasts a winning flavor combination of sweet cherry tomatoes, salty anchovies and Kalamata olives.

INGREDIENTS

For the tart:
1 sheet puff pastry, thawed according to package instructions

For the filling:
60 cherry tomatoes (2 colors are recommended), halved
20 anchovy filets
15 Kalamata olives, pitted and halved

For serving:
10 basil leaves, cut into strips

PREPARATION

1. Preheat the oven to 400°F. Line a baking sheet with parchment paper.

2. Lay the pastry on parchment paper.

3. Place cherry tomatoes on pastry, sliced side up, to within 3/4 inch of edges. Arrange anchovies and olives on top of the tomatoes.

4. Bake for 20-25 minutes, until golden brown. Sprinkle with basil and serve.

✱ The tart can be stored in an airtight container in refrigerator for up to 3 days. Reheating in the oven is recommended prior to serving.

¤ *Spinach Phyllo Pie*

SPINACH PHYLLO PIE

SERVES 6-8

Even though many cooks fear it, phyllo pastry is actually quite easy to work with. Just make sure to keep It covered with a towel or plastic wrap so that it won't dry out and break.

INGREDIENTS

For the pie:
7 squares of phyllo pastry, thawed according to package instructions
6 tablespoons melted butter
4 oz. mozzarella cheese, shredded
3 oz. feta cheese, crumbled
1 large egg
Ground black pepper, to taste

For the filling:
1 tablespoon olive oil
12 oz. fresh spinach

For the topping:
2 tablespoons sesame seeds

PREPARATION

1. Preheat the oven to 350°F.

2. Prepare the filling: Heat a large pan over medium heat, add olive oil and spinach and cook for 3-4 minutes, stirring occasionally, until the spinach wilts. Cool slightly. Press any liquid from cooked spinach by hand and chop coarsely. Combine remaining filling ingredients in a bowl and stir in spinach. There is no need to salt – the cheese adds enough saltiness.

3. Assemble the pie and bake: Place phyllo pastry on a work surface. Brush first layer with butter, top with a second layer and brush that with butter. Repeat this process until all seven layers have been brushed and layered one on top of the other. Place the filling lengthwise along the pastry, fold pastry edges in on both sides and roll into a thick log. With a sharp knife, mark stripes diagonally along the log, 1 1/2 inches apart. Brush with butter and sprinkle with sesame seeds.

4. Bake for 30-35 minutes, until deep golden brown.

✱ The pie can be stored in an airtight container in refrigerator for up to 3 days. Reheating in the oven is recommended prior to serving.

SAVORY ZUCCHINI & WALNUT BREAD

FOR A 9 X 5-INCH
LOAF PAN

Juicy zucchini makes this bread especially moist.

INGREDIENTS

$1^1/_2$ cups all-purpose flour
1 teaspoon sugar
1 teaspoon salt
1 teaspoon baking powder
$^1/_2$ teaspoon baking soda
2 eggs
1 cup plain yogurt
$^1/_2$ cup canola oil
$1^1/_2$ cups zucchini, shredded
1 cup walnuts, coarsely chopped

PREPARATION

1. Preheat the oven to 350°F and grease baking pan.

2. Mix flour, sugar, salt, baking powder and baking soda in a bowl.

3. In a separate bowl, beat eggs. Stir in yogurt, canola oil and zucchini. Pour the egg mixture into the flour mixture, add nuts and mix just until moistened. Pour batter into baking pan and smooth top.

4. Bake for 45-55 minutes, until a toothpick inserted into the center of the loaf comes out clean.

✱ The bread can be stored in an airtight container at room temperature for up to 2 days, or in refrigerator for up to 4 days.

CORN & PEPPER EMPANADAS

MAKES 36 EMPANADAS

These South American pastries are stuffed with a light and colorful vegetarian corn filling.

INGREDIENTS

For the filling:
2 tablespoons olive oil
1 1/2 cups frozen corn kernels, thawed
1 medium onion, finely chopped
1 medium red pepper, finely chopped
5 oz. mozzarella cheese, shredded
1/4 cup cilantro, finely chopped
Salt and ground black pepper, to taste

For the pastry:
4 sheets (34.6 oz.) puff pastry, thawed according to package directions

For glazing:
1 egg
1 tablespoon milk

PREPARATION

1. Preheat the oven to 350°F and line two baking sheets with parchment paper.

2. Prepare the filling: Add olive oil, corn, onion and red pepper to a large skillet over medium heat and sauté for 5 minutes, until onion and pepper soften. Remove from heat and cool for 5 minutes.

3. Stir in cheese and cilantro. Season with salt and pepper to taste.

4. Assemble, fill and bake: Place pastry sheets on work surface and cut out 3-inch circles. Place a heaping teaspoon of filling in the center of each circle and fold in half. Firmly pinch edges together. Place on baking sheets. Beat egg and milk together and brush empanadas.

5. Bake for 20-25 minutes, until golden brown.

✳ The empanadas can be stored in an airtight container in refrigerator for up to 3 days. Reheating in the oven is recommended prior to serving.

SOUPS

GAZPACHO

SERVES 4-6

Thick, red and teeming with flavors, it's best to serve this gazpacho thoroughly chilled on especially hot days.

INGREDIENTS

2 cups tomato juice
5 medium ripe tomatoes, coarsely chopped
2 medium cucumbers, coarsely chopped
1 large red pepper, coarsely chopped
1 medium red onion, coarsely chopped
2–3 garlic cloves, crushed
1 hot green pepper (optional)

$1/3$ cup olive oil
2 tablespoons white wine vinegar
2 tablespoons lemon juice
Salt and ground black pepper, to taste

For serving:
$1/2$ medium cucumber, thinly sliced

PREPARATION

1. Blend the ingredients in a food processor or an immersion blender until smooth.

2. Transfer to the refrigerator for at least 2 hours so the flavors can integrate.

3. Remove from the refrigerator, taste and adjust seasoning with salt and pepper.

4. Ladle into bowls, place a slice of cucumber in the center and serve.

✱ Gazpacho can be stored in an airtight container in refrigerator for up to 3 days.

¤ *Gazpacho*

CAULIFLOWER SOUP

SERVES 4-6

A winter soup with a velvety texture.

INGREDIENTS

2 tablespoons olive oil
1 medium onion, coarsely chopped
2 garlic cloves, coarsely chopped
1 medium cauliflower, cut into small florets
1 medium potato, peeled and cut into $1/2$-inch cubes
4 cups water
Salt and ground black pepper, to taste
1 cup half and half

For serving:
$1/4$ cup cilantro, coarsely chopped

PREPARATION

1. Heat a Dutch oven over medium heat, add olive oil, onion and garlic and sauté for 5 minutes, stirring continuously, until onion and garlic soften.

2. Add cauliflower, potato, water, salt and pepper and bring to a boil. Reduce heat, cover and cook for 20 minutes, until the cauliflower and potato are tender.

3. Add half and half and blend soup with an immersion blender until smooth. Bring to a boil once again, taste and adjust seasoning with salt and pepper.

4. Ladle into bowls, sprinkle with cilantro and serve.

✳ The soup can be stored in an airtight container in refrigerator for up to 3 days.

ROASTED TOMATO SOUP

SERVES 4-6

The roasted tomatoes give this soup its unique flavor.

INGREDIENTS

10 medium plum tomatoes or 8 medium regular tomatoes, sliced in half
4 tablespoons olive oil
1 medium onion, coarsely chopped
4 garlic cloves, coarsely chopped
2 celery ribs, chopped
2 medium carrots, thinly sliced
3 cups water
Salt and ground black pepper, to taste
$1/2$ cup whipping cream

For serving:
$1/4$ cup chives, finely chopped

PREPARATION

1. Preheat the oven to 400°F and line a baking pan with parchment paper. Place the halved tomatoes on the baking pan, sliced side up and sprinkle with 1 tablespoon of olive oil (reserve the remaining olive oil for the soup).

2. Roast the tomatoes for 35-40 minutes, until tender and lightly browned.

3. Heat a Dutch oven over medium heat, add the remaining 3 tablespoons of olive oil, onion, garlic, celery and carrot and cook for 10 minutes, stirring continuously, until the vegetables soften.

4. Add roasted tomatoes, water, salt and pepper and bring to a boil. Reduce heat and cook for 15 minutes.

5. Add cream and blend with an immersion blender until smooth. Bring to boil once again, taste and adjust seasoning with salt and pepper.

6. Ladle into bowls, sprinkle with chives and serve.

✱ The soup can be stored in an airtight container in refrigerator for up to 3 days.

¤ *Spring Minestrone*

SPRING MINESTRONE

SERVES 8

The beans traditionally used in minestrone are replaced with fresh spring peas.

INGREDIENTS

$1/3$ cup olive oil

2 medium onions, coarsely chopped

4 garlic cloves, coarsely chopped

2 medium carrots, peeled and cut into $1/4$-inch cubes

2 celery ribs, cut into $1/4$-inch cubes

2 medium potatoes, peeled and cut into $1/2$-inch cubes

3 medium tomatoes, cut into $1/2$-inch cubes

$1/4$ cup tomato paste

1 cup parsley, coarsely chopped

$1/4$ cup basil, coarsely chopped

9 cups water

2 cups shelled fresh green peas

$1 1/2$ cups pasta

Salt and ground black pepper, to taste

For serving:

Olive oil

PREPARATION

1. Heat a Dutch oven over medium heat, add the olive oil, onion, garlic, carrot and celery and sauté for 10 minutes, stirring occasionally, until the vegetables soften. Add potatoes, tomatoes, tomato paste, parsley, basil and water and bring to a boil.

2. Reduce heat, cover and cook for 20-25 minutes, until the potatoes are tender. Add peas, pasta, salt and pepper and bring to boil again. Cook for 5 minutes, until the pasta is cooked *al dente*. (If you aren't serving the soup immediately, cook the pasta separately and add to soup upon serving). Taste and adjust seasoning with salt and pepper.

3. Ladle into bowls, drizzle with a small amount of olive oil and serve.

✱ The soup can be stored in an airtight container in refrigerator for up to 3 days.

RIBOLLITA (TUSCAN BEAN SOUP)

SERVES 8

A rustic peasant soup that makes use of day-old Italian bread.

INGREDIENTS

1/3 cup olive oil

1 large onion, coarsely chopped

4 garlic cloves, coarsely chopped

2 medium carrots, peeled and cut into 1/2-inch cubes

2 celery ribs, cut into 1/2-inch cubes

4 medium tomatoes, cut into 1/2-inch cubes

1 cup parsley, coarsely chopped

2 medium potatoes, peeled and cut into 1/2-inch cubes

9 cups water

2 cups cooked white beans

3 cups black leaf kale (Cavolo Nero) or fresh spinach, coarsely chopped

1/2 ciabatta bread loaf, 2 days old and broken into pieces

Salt and ground black pepper, to taste

For serving:

Olive oil

PREPARATION

1. Heat a Dutch oven over medium heat, add the olive oil, onion, garlic, carrot and celery and cook for 10 minutes, stirring occasionally, until the vegetables soften.

2. Add tomatoes and parsley and cook for an additional 5 minutes, until the tomatoes are tender.

3. Add potatoes and water and bring to a boil. Reduce heat, cover and cook for 15 minutes.

4. Add beans and cook for 15 minutes, until the potatoes are tender.

5. Add black leaf kale or spinach, ciabatta bread and salt and pepper, stir and reduce heat. Taste and adjust seasoning with salt and pepper.

6. Ladle into bowls, drizzle with a small amount of olive oil and serve.

✳ The soup can be stored in an airtight container in refrigerator for up to 3 days.

EGGPLANT-YOGURT SOUP

SERVES 6

The ultimate Balkan combination of eggplant and yogurt thrives in this soup.

INGREDIENTS

4 medium eggplants
3 tablespoons butter
1 medium onion, coarsely chopped
3 garlic cloves, coarsely chopped
3 cups water
Salt and ground black pepper, to taste
1 1/2 cups plain Greek-style yogurt

For serving:
3 oz. feta cheese, crumbled

PREPARATION

1. Roast the eggplant: Preheat oven to 400°F. Line a baking sheet with parchment paper. Cut eggplant in half lengthwise and place cut side down on baking sheet. Roast 30 minutes or until softened.

2. Cool for 15 minutes. Scrape out the meat with a spoon into a strainer. Allow to drain for 30 minutes.

3. Prepare the soup: Melt butter in a saucepan over medium-low heat, add the onion and garlic and sauté for 5 minutes while stirring, until the onion and garlic are tender. (Take care not to burn the garlic!)

4. Add meat of eggplant, water, salt and pepper and bring to a boil. Reduce heat, cover and cook for 15 minutes.

5. Remove from heat and blend soup with an immersion blender until smooth. Gradually stir in yogurt, taste and adjust seasoning with salt and pepper.

6. Ladle into bowls, sprinkle with feta cheese and serve.

∗ The soup can be stored in an airtight container in refrigerator for up to 3 days.

CARROT-CURRY SOUP

SERVES 3-4

Curry powder is a mixture of spices (cumin, ginger, pepper, turmeric, cardamom and cloves) with a golden brown color. It gives the soup a delicate spiciness that sets off the sweetness of the carrots. Curry powder can be found in your local grocery or specialty food shops.

INGREDIENTS

2 tablespoons olive oil
1 large onion, coarsely chopped
4 garlic cloves, coarsely chopped
6 medium carrots, cut into $1/2$-inch slices
3 cups water
1–2 teaspoons curry powder
1 teaspoon light brown sugar
Salt and ground black pepper, to taste

For serving:
$1/2$ cup yogurt
$1/4$ cup cilantro, coarsely chopped

PREPARATION

1. Heat a large saucepan over medium heat, add the olive oil, onion and garlic and sauté for 5 minutes, stirring occasionally, until the onion is soft.

2. Add carrot, water, curry powder, sugar, salt and pepper and bring to a boil.

3. Reduce heat, cover and cook for 30-40 minutes, until the carrots are tender.

4. Blend the soup with an immersion blender until smooth. If the soup is too thick, add a small amount of boiling water. Taste and adjust seasoning with salt and pepper.

5. Ladle into bowls, drizzle each serving with a teaspoon of yogurt, sprinkle with cilantro and serve.

* The soup can be stored in an airtight container in refrigerator for up to 3 days.

¤ *Carrot-Curry Soup*

¤ *Couscous, Tomato & Spinach Soup*

COUSCOUS, TOMATO & SPINACH SOUP

SERVES 6

A very thick, stew-like soup that you'll want to make over and over again.

INGREDIENTS

2 tablespoons olive oil
1 large onion, coarsely chopped
3 garlic cloves, coarsely chopped
6 large tomatoes, coarsely chopped
$4^1/_2$ cups water
Salt and ground black pepper, to taste
$^3/_4$ cup couscous (whole-wheat is preferable)
2 cups fresh spinach leaves, coarsely chopped

PREPARATION

1. Heat a Dutch oven over medium heat, add the olive oil, onion and garlic and sauté for 5 minutes, until the onion and garlic are tender.

2. Add tomatoes, water, salt and pepper and bring to a boil. Reduce heat, cover and cook for 10 minutes.

3. Add couscous, bring to a boil again and cook for 5 minutes uncovered, until the couscous is tender.

4. Remove from heat, add spinach and stir. Taste and adjust seasoning with salt and pepper.

✳ The soup can be stored in an airtight container in refrigerator for up to 3 days. The couscous will continue to absorb liquid and the soup will become thicker as time passes. It can be diluted with water, as needed.

BROCCOLI SOUP

SERVES 4-6

Fresh, green and great for your health.

INGREDIENTS

3 tablespoons olive oil

2 medium onions, coarsely chopped

6 garlic cloves, coarsely chopped

2 medium heads of broccoli, cut into small florets

5 cups water

Salt and ground black pepper, to taste

PREPARATION

1. Heat a Dutch oven over medium heat, add the olive oil, onion and garlic and sauté for 5 minutes, until the onion and garlic soften.

2. Add broccoli, water, salt and pepper and bring to a boil. Reduce heat, cover and cook for 15 minutes, until the broccoli is crisp-tender.

3. Blend the soup with an immersion blender until smooth. Taste and adjust seasoning with salt and pepper.

✱ The soup can be stored in an airtight container in refrigerator for up to 3 days.

PEA & MINT SOUP

SERVES 4-6

Cook the peas only until they soften — light cooking maintains their flavor and green color.

INGREDIENTS

3 tablespoons olive oil

2 medium onions, coarsely chopped

6 garlic cloves, coarsely chopped

1 cup mint, coarsely chopped

6 cups shelled fresh green peas

4 cups water

Salt and ground black pepper, to taste

PREPARATION

1. Heat a Dutch oven over medium heat, add the onion and garlic and sauté for 10 minutes until the onions and garlic soften.

2. Add mint and cook for a minute, stirring continuously.

3. Add peas, water, salt and pepper and bring to a boil. Reduce heat, cover and cook for 6-8 minutes, just until the peas are tender.

4. Blend the soup with an immersion blender until smooth. Taste and adjust seasoning with salt and pepper.

✱ The soup can be stored in an airtight container in refrigerator for up to 3 days.

MUSHROOM SOUP

SERVES 6

The secret to this soup is blending a third of it. This results in a thick consistency and rich taste, without having to add a single drop of cream!

INGREDIENTS

¹/₄ cup olive oil

2 medium onions, finely chopped

16 oz. mushrooms (using two varieties is best), cut into ¹/₄-inch thick slices

8 oz. dried mushrooms, soaked in 1 cup boiling water

2 medium potatoes, peeled and shredded

4 cups water

Salt and ground black pepper, to taste

For serving:

Small bunch parsley, chopped

PREPARATION

1. Heat a Dutch oven over medium heat, add the olive oil and onion and sauté for 5 minutes, stirring occasionally, until golden brown.

2. Add fresh mushrooms and cook for 5 minutes while stirring, until the mushrooms start to soften.

3. Remove dried mushrooms from soaking water, coarsely chop them and transfer to the Dutch oven, along with the soaking water.

4. Add potatoes, water, salt and pepper and bring to a boil. Reduce heat, cover and cook for 15 minutes, until the potatoes are tender.

5. Separate out a third of the soup and blend in a blender or with an immersion blender. Return to Dutch oven and stir, taste and adjust seasoning with salt and pepper.

6. Ladle into bowls, sprinkle with parsley and serve.

∗ The soup can be stored in an airtight container in refrigerator for up to 3 days.

ONION SOUP

SERVES 4

Red wine and apple juice provide this soup with a deep flavor and intense color.

INGREDIENTS

2 tablespoons butter
6 large onions, halved and cut into $1/4$-inch thick slices
2 tablespoons flour
$1/2$ cup red wine
$1/2$ cup apple juice
5 cups water
Salt and ground black pepper, to taste

For serving:
1 tablespoon thyme leaves

PREPARATION

1. Melt butter in a Dutch oven over medium heat, add onion and sauté for 10 minutes, stirring occasionally, until golden brown.

2. Add flour and wine, stir and cook for a minute until the wine evaporates.

3. Add apple juice, water, salt and pepper and bring to a boil. Reduce heat, cover and cook for 20 minutes, until the onion is tender. Taste and adjust seasoning with salt and pepper.

4. Ladle into bowls, sprinkle with thyme and serve.

✶ The soup can be stored in an airtight container in refrigerator for up to 3 days.

RED LENTIL, CARROT & GREEN ONION SOUP

SERVES 6-8

The main advantage of red lentils, other than their nutritional value, is that they cook in just a few minutes. So you can make a rich, almost stew-like soup in less than 20 minutes.

INGREDIENTS

$1/4$ cup olive oil
1 large onion, finely chopped
3 medium carrots, peeled and shredded
2 cups red lentils, rinsed and drained
8 cups water
Salt and ground black pepper, to taste
8 green onions, cut into $1/2$-inch thick slices

PREPARATION

1. Heat a Dutch oven over medium heat, add olive oil, onion and carrots and sauté for 6-8 minutes, stirring occasionally, until onion and carrots are tender.

2. Add lentils, water, salt and black pepper and bring to a boil. Reduce heat, cover and cook for 8-10 minutes, until the lentils are tender. Add green onion, stir and cook for another minute. Taste and adjust seasoning with salt and pepper.

✱ The soup can be stored in an airtight container in refrigerator for up to 3 days.

¤ *Red Lentil, Carrot & Green Onion Soup*

¤ *Beet & Potato Soup*

BEET & POTATO SOUP

SERVES 6-8

This recipe takes the classic Russian borscht and gives it a twist with Chinese five spice. An entirely different soup emerges.

INGREDIENTS

$1/4$ cup olive oil
2 medium onions, finely chopped
4 garlic cloves, coarsely chopped
4 medium beets, peeled and cut into $1/2$-inch cubes
4 medium potatoes, peeled and cut into 1-inch cubes
8 cups water
1 teaspoon Chinese five spice powder
Salt and ground black pepper, to taste

For serving:
Sour cream

PREPARATION

1. Heat a Dutch oven over medium heat, add olive oil, onion and garlic and sauté for 5 minutes, stirring occasionally, until onion and garlic soften.

2. Add beets, potatoes, water, five spice powder, salt and black pepper and bring to a boil. Reduce heat, cover and simmer for 60 minutes, until the beets and potatoes are tender. Remove a third of soup and blend it in a blender or using an immersion blender. Return the blended third to the Dutch oven, stir, taste and adjust seasoning with salt and pepper.

3. Ladle into bowls, drizzle each serving with a teaspoon of sour cream and serve.

✻ The soup can be stored in an airtight container in refrigerator for up to 3 days.

SWEET POTATO & CHICKPEA SOUP

SERVES 4-6

This popular sweet potato soup is given a healthy and tasty reinforcement of chickpeas.

INGREDIENTS

$1/4$ cup olive oil
1 large onion, finely chopped
4 garlic cloves, coarsely chopped
2 medium sweet potatoes, cut into $1/2$-inch cubes
3 cups cooked chickpeas
6 cups water
Salt and ground black pepper, to taste

PREPARATION

1. Heat a Dutch oven over medium heat, add olive oil, onion and garlic and cook for around 5 minutes, stirring occasionally, until onion and garlic are tender.

2. Add sweet potatoes, chickpeas, water, salt and black pepper and bring to a boil. Reduce heat, cover and cook for 15-20 minutes, until the sweet potato is soft.

3. Remove a third of soup and blend it in a blender or using an immersion blender. Return the blended third to pot, stir, taste and adjust seasoning with salt and pepper.

✳ The soup can be stored in an airtight container in refrigerator for up to 3 days.

ZUCCHINI & PESTO SOUP

SERVES 4-6

This flavorful and colorful summer soup can be served hot or cold.

INGREDIENTS

$1/4$ cup olive oil
1 large onion, finely chopped
3 garlic cloves, coarsely chopped
4 medium zucchini, shredded
4 cups water
$1/3$ cup pesto
Salt and ground black pepper, to taste

For serving:
Sour cream

PREPARATION

1. Heat a Dutch oven over medium heat, add olive oil, onion, garlic and zucchini and sauté for 5 minutes, stirring occasionally, until onion, garlic and zucchini start to soften.

2. Add water, pesto, salt and black pepper and bring to a boil. Reduce heat, cover and cook for 15 minutes, until the zucchini is tender. Remove a third of soup and blend it in a blender or using an immersion blender. Return the blended third to the Dutch oven, stir, taste and adjust seasoning with salt and pepper.

3. Serve with sour cream.

✱ The soup can be stored in an airtight container in refrigerator for up to 3 days.

SIDE
DISHES

PROVENÇAL VEGETABLE TIAN

SERVES 4

Like Ratatouille, this dish is vegetable-based and comes from Provençe. However, in this case the vegetables are layered and oven-baked, rather than pan-fried.

INGREDIENTS

4 tablespoons olive oil
1 large onion, finely diced
Salt and ground black pepper, to taste
1 long eggplant, cut into $\frac{1}{8}$-inch thick slices
3 plum tomatoes, cut into $\frac{1}{8}$-inch thick slices
1 medium zucchini, cut into $\frac{1}{8}$-inch thick slices
1 sprig thyme, leaves only

PREPARATION

1. Preheat oven to 350°F.

2. Heat a medium skillet over medium heat. Add 2 tablespoons olive oil (set aside remaining olive oil for baking), onion, salt and pepper and sauté for 5 minutes, stirring continuously, until the onion softens.

3. Distribute cooked onion in a single layer in a 12-inch ovenproof baking dish. Arrange vegetables in alternating, overlapping layers (eggplant, tomato, zucchini), in a circular pattern. Sprinkle with salt and pepper and drizzle with remaining 2 tablespoons of olive oil.

4. Bake for 30 minutes. Sprinkle with thyme and bake for another 30 minutes, until golden.

* The tian can be stored in an airtight container in refrigerator for up to 3 days. Reheat in microwave.

¤ *Provençal Vegetable Tian*

¤ *Roasted Carrots in Maple Syrup with Red Pepper Flakes*

ROASTED CARROTS IN MAPLE SYRUP WITH RED PEPPER FLAKES

SERVES 6-8

A sweet and spicy take on the common carrot.

INGREDIENTS

10 medium yellow and
  orange carrots, peeled
  and sliced in half
  lengthwise
1/3 cup real maple syrup
1 1/2 teaspoons red pepper
  flakes
Sea salt, to taste

PREPARATION

1. Preheat the oven to
400°F and grease a baking
pan.

2. Place carrots in the
baking pan. Add syrup,
then sprinkle with chili and
sea salt and toss.

3. Bake for 30-40 minutes,
turning once during
cooking, until golden brown.

* Carrots can be stored
in an airtight container in
refrigerator for up to
3 days. Reheat in a 350°F
oven.

SWEET POTATOES IN SOY WITH SESAME SEEDS

SERVES 4-6

An irresistible flavor combination:

salty, tart, sweet and spicy.

INGREDIENTS

3 medium sweet potatoes,
  peeled and cut into
  1 1/2-inch cubes

For the sauce:
3 tablespoons soy sauce
2 tablespoons balsamic
  vinegar
2 tablespoons honey
4 teaspoons sesame
  seeds
2 garlic cloves, crushed
Ground black pepper,
  to taste

PREPARATION

1. Preheat oven to 400°F
and grease a baking pan.

2. Mix sauce ingredients
in a bowl. Place sweet
potatoes in baking pan, add
sauce and stir.

3. Bake for 35-45 minutes,
stirring once or twice
during cooking, until golden
brown.

* Potatoes can be stored
in an airtight container in
refrigerator for up to
3 days. Reheat in a 350°F
oven.

GLAZED RED ONIONS

SERVES 6-8

Onions are usually a member of the backup chorus, used to strengthen the overall flavor of a dish. In this recipe, onions are featured center stage as the star of the dish.

INGREDIENTS

10 medium red onions, quartered

For the sauce:
2 tablespoons dry red wine
2 tablespoons canola oil
2 tablespoons dark brown sugar
2 tablespoons balsamic vinegar
Salt and ground black pepper, to taste

PREPARATION

1. Preheat oven to 400°F and grease a baking pan.

2. Mix sauce ingredients in a bowl. Place onions in baking pan, add sauce and stir. Cover with aluminum foil.

3. Bake for 30 minutes. Remove aluminum foil and bake for another 30 minutes, stirring once or twice during baking, until onions have browned and softened.

∗ The onions can be stored in an airtight container in refrigerator for up to 3 days. Reheat in a 350°F oven.

CHEESE-STUFFED MUSHROOMS

SERVES 4-6

Mushrooms are elegant little cups for this cheese mixture — resulting in a classic hors d'oeuvre.

INGREDIENTS

20 large button mushrooms or 30 small portobello mushrooms, stems removed

For the filling:
5 oz. feta cheese, crumbled
5 oz. Roquefort cheese, crumbled
1/2 cup pecans, coarsely chopped
1/4 cup breadcrumbs
1/4 cup basil, chopped

PREPARATION

1. Preheat oven to 400°F and grease a baking pan.

2. Mix filling ingredients in a bowl. Stuff button mushrooms with filling or place a mound on portobello mushrooms. Place stuffed mushrooms in baking pan.

3. Bake for 10-15 minutes, until lightly golden.

∗ The mushrooms can be stored in an airtight container in refrigerator for up to 3 days. Reheat in a 350°F oven.

CABBAGE & BRUSSELS SPROUTS GRATIN

SERVES 6-8

Cabbage and Brussels sprouts are extra tasty when baked in a seasoned, creamy casserole.

INGREDIENTS

1 pound Brussels sprouts

1½ cups half and half

3 garlic cloves, crushed

2 sprigs thyme, leaves only

Pinch of freshly ground
   nutmeg

Salt and ground black
   pepper, to taste

Half of a medium green
   cabbage, sliced into
   8 wedges

4 oz. mozzarella cheese,
   shredded

2 oz. Parmesan cheese,
   finely grated

PREPARATION

1. Preheat oven to 400°F and grease a baking pan that has sides at least 2 inches high.

2. Cook Brussels sprouts for 2-3 minutes in salted boiling water, until barely tender. Drain well.

3. Heat the half and half, garlic, thyme, nutmeg, salt and pepper in a small saucepan, while stirring occasionally. Bring to a simmer, then remove from heat. Taste and adjust seasoning with salt and pepper.

4. Place cabbage and Brussels sprouts in baking pan. Add half and half mixture, sprinkle with cheeses and cover with aluminum foil.

5. Bake for 45 minutes. Remove aluminum foil and bake for another 20 minutes, until golden.

* The gratin can be stored in an airtight container in refrigerator for up to 3 days. Reheat in a 350°F oven.

¤ *Roasted Asparagus with Pesto Aioli*

ROASTED ASPARAGUS WITH PESTO AIOLI

SERVES 4-6

Asparagus is tastier when roasted in the oven, especially when it gets this velvety coating of pesto aioli.

INGREDIENTS

For the aioli:
2 egg yolks
1 large garlic clove, crushed
1–1½ teaspoons smooth Dijon mustard
1 tablespoon white wine vinegar
1 tablespoon lemon juice
1 heaping tablespoon pesto
Salt and ground black pepper, to taste
½ cup canola oil
¼ cup olive oil

For the asparagus:
1 bunch asparagus, trimmed
1 tablespoon olive oil
Salt and ground black pepper, to taste

PREPARATION

1. Prepare the pesto aioli: Whisk yolks, garlic, mustard, vinegar, lemon juice, pesto and a small amount of salt and pepper in the top of a double boiler. Place over simmering water, whisking constantly until mixture reaches 160°F, about 2 minutes. Immediately remove top of double boiler from heat. Drizzle in both oils slowly, while whisking, until well blended. Taste and adjust seasoning with salt and pepper. Pesto aioli can be stored in an airtight container in refrigerator for up to 3 days.

2. Prepare the asparagus: Preheat oven to 350°F and line a baking sheet with parchment paper. Place asparagus on baking sheet in a single layer, drizzle with olive oil and season with salt and pepper. Bake for 15-20 minutes, until asparagus starts to brown and soften.

3. Serve: Place the asparagus on a serving platter and drizzle with half of the aioli.

✻ The asparagus dish can be stored in an airtight container in refrigerator for up to 3 days. Reheat in a 350°F oven.

✻ Use the remaining aioli with other meat or vegetables dishes, as a dip or spread onto sandwiches.

VEGETABLE GRATIN

SERVES 6

A lighter and more colorful version of the classic potato gratin.

INGREDIENTS

1 medium head of broccoli, cut into small florets
2 medium carrots, peeled and cut into $1/2$-inch thick slices
$1^1/_2$ cups half and half
3 garlic cloves, crushed
2 sprigs thyme, leaves only
Pinch of freshly ground nutmeg
Salt and ground black pepper, to taste
2 medium zucchini, cut into $1/2$-inch thick slices
8 oz. mozzarella cheese, shredded

PREPARATION

1. Preheat oven to 350°F and grease a baking pan with at least 2-inch high sides.

2. Cook broccoli and carrots for 3-4 minutes in salted boiling water, until crisp-tender. Drain well.

3. Heat the half and half, garlic, thyme, nutmeg, salt and pepper in a small saucepan, while stirring occasionally. Bring to a simmer, then remove from heat. Taste and adjust seasoning.

4. Place broccoli, carrots and zucchini in baking pan. Add half and half mixture and sprinkle with cheese.

5. Bake for 35-40 minutes, until golden.

* The gratin can be stored in an airtight container in refrigerator for up to 3 days. Reheat in a 350°F oven.

RATATOUILLE

SERVES 6

A French dish from Provençe featuring fresh summer vegetables.

INGREDIENTS

1/3 cup olive oil

2 medium onions, cut into
  1/2-inch cubes

4 garlic cloves, coarsely chopped

2 sprigs thyme, chopped

2 medium red peppers, cut into
  1-inch cubes

2 medium zucchini, cut into
  1-inch cubes

1 medium eggplant, cut into
  1-inch cubes

4 tomatoes, cut into 1-inch cubes

3/4 cup water

1 heaping tablespoon tomato paste

2 bay leaves

Salt and ground black pepper, to taste

For serving:

1/3 cup basil, chopped

PREPARATION

1. Heat a Dutch oven over medium heat, add olive oil, onion, garlic and thyme and sauté for 5 minutes, stirring occasionally, until onion and garlic soften. Add the vegetables, water, tomato paste, bay leaves, salt and pepper and bring to a boil.

2. Reduce heat and cook uncovered for 15-20 minutes, stirring occasionally, until the vegetables are tender. Taste and adjust seasoning with salt and pepper.

3. Sprinkle with basil and serve.

∗ Ratatouille can be stored in an airtight container in refrigerator for up to 3 days. Reheat in microwave.

LEMON-GARLIC OKRA

SERVES 4

It's best to use small okra — its more appealing texture is sure to win this vegetable some new fans.

INGREDIENTS

3 tablespoons olive oil
1 pound fresh small okra, stems removed
$1/4$ cup water
3 tablespoons lemon juice
2–3 garlic cloves, crushed
Salt and ground black pepper, to taste

For serving:
1 tablespoon lemon juice
$1/4$ cup parsley, coarsely chopped

PREPARATION

1. Heat a large skillet over medium heat, add the olive oil and okra and sauté for 2 minutes, while stirring.

2. Add water, lemon juice, garlic, salt and pepper and bring to a boil.

3. Reduce heat and cook for 5 minutes, until the okra softens, but is still firm. Taste and adjust seasoning with salt and pepper.

4. Remove from heat, drizzle with tablespoon of lemon juice, sprinkle with chopped parsley and serve.

✳ This okra dish can be stored in an airtight container in refrigerator for up to 3 days. Reheat in microwave.

HONEY-GARLIC ROASTED EGGPLANT

SERVES 4

In this recipe the eggplant is treated to a healthy dose of everything that makes a vegetable dish great: olive oil, honey, garlic and thyme.

INGREDIENTS

1 large eggplant, cut into 1-inch cubes
$1/4$ cup olive oil
2 tablespoons honey
5 garlic cloves, peeled and halved
2 sprigs thyme, chopped
Salt and black pepper, to taste

PREPARATION

1. Preheat oven to 350°F and line baking pan with parchment paper.

2. Toss the eggplant, olive oil, honey, garlic, thyme, salt and pepper in a bowl. Place in baking pan.

3. Bake for 30 minutes, stirring once or twice during cooking, until golden.

✳ This eggplant dish can be stored in an airtight container in refrigerator for up to 3 days. Reheat in a 350°F oven.

¤ *Honey-Garlic Roasted Eggplant*

TRI-COLORED OVEN-ROASTED PEPPERS

SERVES 4-6

A colorful, summery dish that's easy to prepare.

INGREDIENTS

16 small peppers (at least 3 different colors)
3 tablespoons olive oil
2 tablespoons balsamic vinegar
1 sprig thyme, leaves only
Salt and ground black pepper, to taste

PREPARATION

1. Preheat oven to 350°F and grease a baking pan.

2. Toss peppers, olive oil, balsamic vinegar, thyme, salt and pepper in a bowl. Place on baking sheet.

3. Bake for 30-35 minutes, turning once or twice during cooking, until lightly browned.

✱ The peppers can be stored in an airtight container in refrigerator for up to 3 days. Reheat in microwave.

¤ *Tri-Colored Oven-Roasted Peppers*

CHEESE-STUFFED TOMATOES

SERVES 6

For rustic-looking stuffed tomatoes keep the stem and part of the vine attached.

INGREDIENTS

6 large tomatoes, sliced in half
6 oz. Parmesan cheese, finely grated
8 oz. feta cheese, crumbled
14 Kalamata olives, pitted and sliced in half
2 green onions, thinly sliced
1/4 cup panko (Japanese breadcrumbs)

PREPARATION

1. Preheat oven to 350°F and grease a baking pan.

2. Remove all liquids and seeds from tomatoes, leaving only the meaty part behind. Place in baking pan.

3. Mix cheeses, olives and green onion in a bowl. Fill the tomatoes and sprinkle the tops with panko.

4. Bake for 25-30 minutes, until golden.

✱ The tomatoes can be stored in an airtight container in refrigerator for up to 3 days. Reheat in a 350°F oven.

OVEN-ROASTED POTATOES, ONIONS & MUSHROOMS

SERVES 4-6

Potatoes might just be the ultimate side dish, and with the addition of mushrooms, onions and rosemary they soar to new heights.

INGREDIENTS

5 medium potatoes, peeled and cut into wedges
1 pound mushrooms (two varieties are recommended)
2 medium onions, sliced in $1/4$-inch rings
1 sprig rosemary, leaves only
$1/4$ cup olive oil
Salt and ground black pepper, to taste

PREPARATION

1. Preheat oven to 400°F and grease a baking pan.

2. Mix potatoes, mushrooms, onions, rosemary, olive oil, salt and pepper in a bowl. Place in baking pan and cover with aluminum foil.

3. Bake for 45 minutes. Remove aluminum foil and bake for another 30 minutes, until golden brown.

✱ The dish can be stored in an airtight container in refrigerator for up to 3 days. Reheat in a 350°F oven.

¤ *Oven-Roasted Potatoes, Onions & Mushrooms*

SPINACH IN RICOTTA

SERVES 4

This spinach is creamy and rich in flavor without even a drop of cream, thanks to low-fat ricotta cheese.

INGREDIENTS

1 tablespoon olive oil
2 pounds fresh spinach leaves
8 oz. part-skim ricotta cheese
1–2 garlic cloves, crushed
Salt and ground black pepper, to taste

PREPARATION

1. Heat a large skillet over medium heat. Add olive oil and half the spinach and cook for about 2 minutes, stirring occasionally, until the spinach starts to wilt. (The spinach continues wilting even after it is removed from the heat.)

2. Transfer spinach to a plate. Repeat the process with the remaining spinach. (There is no need to add more oil to the pan).

3. Return cooked spinach to the skillet, add ricotta, garlic, salt and pepper and stir. Cook until spinach is tender, stirring frequently. Taste and adjust seasoning with salt and pepper.

✳ The spinach dish can be stored in an airtight container in refrigerator for up to 3 days. Drain off any liquid that has accumulated. Reheat in microwave.

OVEN-ROASTED FENNEL

SERVES 4

As tasty as raw fennel is in a salad, it is just as delicious when roasted.

INGREDIENTS

3 medium fennel bulbs, leaves removed and cut into sixths
2 tablespoons olive oil
1 sprig thyme, leaves only
Salt and ground black pepper, to taste

PREPARATION

1. Preheat oven to 400°F and grease a baking pan.

2. Mix fennel, olive oil, thyme, salt and pepper in baking pan.

3. Bake for 25-30 minutes, stirring once or twice during cooking process, until lightly browned.

✳ The dish can be stored in an airtight container in refrigerator for up to 2 days. Reheat in a 350°F oven.

¤ *Oven-Roasted Fennel*

PUMPKIN & CHICKPEA TAGINE

SERVES 6

*This vegetarian tagine is rich
in flavor due to an abundance
of aromatic herbs.
Serve tagine with rice.*

INGREDIENTS

$1/4$ cup canola oil
2 medium red onions, diced
4 garlic cloves, coarsely chopped
1 large red pepper, cut into $1/2$-inch
    cubes
1 tablespoon sweet paprika
1 teaspoon hot paprika
1 teaspoon ground coriander
1 teaspoon cumin
1 teaspoon cinnamon
28 oz. canned tomatoes, diced

1 cup water
1 tablespoon sugar
Salt, to taste
1 pound pumpkin, peeled and cut into
    1-inch cubes
2 cups chickpeas, cooked

For serving:
$1/4$ cup fresh cilandro, coarsely
    chopped
Cooked rice

PREPARATION

1. Heat a Dutch oven over medium heat, add canola oil, onion, garlic and pepper
and cook for 5 minutes, stirring occasionally, until the vegetables start to soften.

2. Add sweet paprika, hot paprika, ground coriander, cumin and cinnamon. Cook,
while stirring, about 1 minute, until spices become aromatic. Take care not to
burn spices!

3. Add tomatoes, water, sugar and salt and bring to a boil. Add pumpkin and
chickpeas and bring to a boil again. Cook for 15 minutes, until the pumpkin is
tender. Taste and adjust seasoning with salt and pepper.

4. Sprinkle with fresh cilantro and serve with rice.

✳ The tagine can be stored in an airtight container in refrigerator for up to
3 days. Reheat in microwave.

VEGETABLE & YOGURT CURRY

SERVES 4

Thai curries, like this red one, are usually made with coconut milk. By replacing the coconut milk with goat milk yogurt, the dish is lighter and healthier.

INGREDIENTS

2 tablespoons canola oil
1 medium onion, coarsely chopped
2 sweet potatoes, peeled and cut into 1-inch cubes
1–1$\frac{1}{2}$ teaspoons red curry paste
2 cups goat milk yogurt
1 cup vegetable stock
Salt and ground black pepper, to taste
2 cups shelled fresh green peas
10 oz. button mushrooms, sliced in half

For serving:
$\frac{1}{4}$ cup cilantro, coarsely chopped

PREPARATION

1. Heat a saucepan over medium heat. Add canola oil and onion and sauté for 5 minutes, stirring occasionally, until the onion softens. Add sweet potato, curry paste, yogurt, vegetable stock, salt and pepper. Stir and bring to a boil.

2. Reduce heat, cover and cook for 15 minutes.

3. Add peas and mushrooms, stir and bring to a boil again. Cook for 5-7 minutes, until the sweet potatoes are tender. Taste and adjust seasoning with salt and pepper.

4. Sprinkle with chopped cilantro and serve.

✳ Curry can be stored in an airtight container in refrigerator for up to 2 days. Reheat in microwave.

MUSTARD ROASTED CAULIFLOWER

SERVES 4-6

Cauliflower is a versatile vegetable. When roasted with Dijon mustard and a drop of honey, its delicate flavor is only improved.

INGREDIENTS

3 tablespoons olive oil
$1^1/_2$ teaspoons coarse grain Dijon mustard
1 teaspoon honey
Salt and ground black pepper, to taste
1 large cauliflower, separated into large florets

For serving:
1 tablespoon parsley, finely chopped

PREPARATION

1. Preheat the oven to 400°F.

2. Mix olive oil, mustard, honey, salt and black pepper in a bowl. Add cauliflower florets and stir until coated. Place in baking pan.

3. Bake for 40-50 minutes, stirring once, until golden.

4. Sprinkle with parsley and serve.

✱ The cauliflower can be stored in an airtight container in refrigerator for up to 3 days. Reheat in microwave.

¤ *Mustard Roasted Cauliflower*

ASPARAGUS IN LEMON & GARLIC

SERVES 4-6

Oven-roasted asparagus with chunks of lemon and crushed garlic — an amazing side dish that requires virtually no effort.

INGREDIENTS

1 bunch asparagus, trimmed
$1/2$ of a medium lemon, thinly sliced
1 large garlic clove, finely chopped
1 tablespoon olive oil
Coarse salt and ground black pepper, to taste

PREPARATION

1. Preheat the oven to 350°F.

2. Place asparagus on a baking sheet in a single layer. Sprinkle with lemon slices and garlic. Drizzle with olive oil and season with salt and black pepper.

3. Bake for 15-20 minutes, just until the asparagus starts to brown and is tender.

✱ Asparagus can be stored in an airtight container in refrigerator for up to 3 days. Reheat in a 350°F.

BUTTER & THYME ROASTED BEETS

SERVES 4-6

By oven-roasting beets in butter you enhance their earthy, sweet flavor. With this technique, the beets are roasted in an aluminum foil package, baking them in their own steam.

INGREDIENTS

6 medium beets, peeled and cut into quarters
4 tablespoons butter, cut into small cubes
2 sprigs of thyme, leaves only
Salt and ground black pepper, to taste

PREPARATION

1. Preheat the oven to 400°F.

2. Place beets on a large sheet of aluminum foil, sprinkle with cubes of butter and thyme leaves and season with salt and black pepper.

3. Seal the aluminum foil into package and place on a baking sheet.

4. Bake for 30-40 minutes, until the beets are tender.

✳ The beets can be stored in an airtight container in refrigerator for up to 3 days. Reheat in microwave.

PASTA
& GRAINS

¤ *Couscous, Beet & Spinach Salad with Tahini Dressing*

COUSCOUS, BEET & SPINACH SALAD WITH TAHINI DRESSING

SERVES 6-8

A healthy union of super foods: whole-wheat couscous, beets, spinach, nuts and tahini.

INGREDIENTS

12 oz. quick-cooking whole-wheat couscous
2 medium beets, cooked and cut into 1-inch cubes
3 cups fresh spinach, coarsely chopped
1 cup pecans or walnuts, coarsely chopped

For the dressing:
$1/3$ cup tahini
$1/3$ cup lemon juice
$1/4$ cup water
1 teaspoon light brown sugar
Salt and ground black pepper, to taste

PREPARATION

1. Prepare the couscous according to package directions and cool thoroughly. Fluff with a fork to separate grains.

2. Transfer couscous to a large bowl and add beets, spinach and nuts.

3. Mix dressing ingredients well, pour over salad and stir. Taste and adjust seasoning with salt and pepper.

∗ This salad can be stored in an airtight container in refrigerator for up to 3 days.

TABOULEH

SERVES 6

A traditional Eastern Mediterranean bulgur salad with cucumber, tomato and an abundance of fresh herbs.

INGREDIENTS

1 cup fine-grind bulgur wheat
1 medium red onion, very finely diced
1 medium cucumber, finely diced
1 medium tomato, finely diced
1 cup parsley, finely chopped
$1/2$ cup cilantro, finely chopped
$1/2$ cup mint, finely chopped
$1/4$ cup olive oil
$1/4$ cup lemon juice
Salt and ground black pepper, to taste

PREPARATION

1. Soak bulgur in a large bowl of hot water for 30 minutes, until it expands. Drain well.

2. Transfer the bulgur to a dry bowl, add remaining ingredients and mix. Taste and adjust seasoning with salt and pepper.

✻ This salad can be stored in an airtight container in refrigerator for up to 2 days.

ORZO, ZUCCHINI & PINE NUT SALAD

SERVES 6-8

Orzo is rice-shaped pasta. Its small size makes it perfect for mixing into cold salads, like in this recipe.

INGREDIENTS

1 pound orzo pasta
5 tablespoons olive oil
4 medium zucchini, cut into $1/2$-inch cubes
$3/4$ cup pine nuts, lightly toasted
$1/3$ cup chives, finely chopped
3 tablespoons lemon juice
2 tablespoons balsamic vinegar
Salt and ground black pepper, to taste

PREPARATION

1. Cook the orzo: Bring a Dutch oven of salted water to a boil. Add orzo and cook until *al dente*. Drain well, add 2 tablespoons of olive oil and stir to prevent the orzo from sticking. Cool.

2. Prepare the zucchini: Add $1^1/2$ tablespoons of olive oil and half of zucchini to a large skillet over medium-high heat. Sauté for 8-10 minutes, until golden brown. Repeat with remaining $1^1/2$ tablespoons of oil and zucchini.

3. Serve: Combine orzo, zucchini, pine nuts, chives, lemon juice, balsamic vinegar, salt and pepper in a large bowl. Taste and adjust seasoning with salt and pepper.

✱ This salad can be stored in an airtight container in refrigerator for up to 3 days.

¤ *Red Rice, Grape, Carrot & Feta Cheese Salad*

RED RICE, GRAPE, CARROT & FETA CHEESE SALAD

SERVES 4-6

A satisfying salad, rich in colors and flavors, easy to prepare and simply delicious.

INGREDIENTS

2 cups red rice, rinsed and drained (or subsitute brown rice)
2 cups grapes, sliced in half
2 medium carrots, peeled and coarsely grated
4 oz. feta cheese, coarsely crumbled

For the dressing:
1/4 cup olive oil
1/4 cup lemon juice
1 teaspoon honey
1 teaspoon smooth Dijon mustard
Salt and ground black pepper, to taste

PREPARATION

1. Bring a Dutch oven of salted water to a boil. Add red rice and cook for 20-25 minutes until *al dente*. Drain well. Cool.

2. Transfer rice to a bowl. Add grapes, carrot and feta cheese.

3. Mix dressing ingredients well, pour over salad and stir. Taste and adjust seasoning with salt and pepper.

✱ This salad can be stored in an airtight container in refrigerator for up to 3 days.

¤ *Pasta in Tomato, Garlic & Spinach Sauce*

PASTA IN TOMATO, GARLIC & SPINACH SAUCE

SERVES 4-6

A light and tasty sauce made of garlic, with fresh spinach added at the last minute.

INGREDIENTS

For the sauce:
$1/4$ cup olive oil
3 garlic cloves, thinly sliced
8 medium tomatoes (or 6 large tomatoes), cut into 1-inch cubes
Salt and ground black pepper, to taste
2 cups fresh spinach, coarsely chopped

1 pound whole-wheat pasta

For serving:
Shaved fresh Parmesan cheese

PREPARATION

1. Prepare the sauce: Heat a large skillet over medium heat. Add olive oil and garlic and sauté for 2 minutes, stirring continuously, only until the garlic starts to soften. (Take care not to burn it!) Add tomatoes, salt and pepper and cook for 10 minutes, stirring occasionally, until tender. Add spinach and stir. Taste and adjust seasoning with salt and pepper.

2. Cook the pasta: Bring salted water to a boil in a Dutch oven. Add pasta and cook until *al dente*.

3. Serve: Drain pasta, add to sauce and stir. Serve with Parmesan cheese.

✴ This pasta dish can be stored in an airtight container in refrigerator for up to 3 days.

PASTA IN ARUGULA PESTO

SERVES 4-6

This pasta dish features arugula pesto rather than traditional basil pesto. The unique flavor of the arugula gives the dish a peppery mustard kick.

INGREDIENTS

For the sauce:
2 packed cups arugula leaves
$1/2$ cup basil leaves
$1/4$ cup Parmesan cheese, finely grated
$1/4$ cup pine nuts, toasted
2 garlic cloves, crushed
Zest of $1/2$ lemon, finely grated
Salt and ground black pepper, to taste
$1/2$ cup light olive oil

1 pound whole-wheat pasta

PREPARATION

1. Prepare the sauce: Purée the arugula, basil, Parmesan, pine nuts, garlic, lemon zest and a small amount of salt and pepper in the food processor. Slowly add olive oil in a thin stream, while continuing to blend, until a thick sauce forms. Taste and adjust seasoning with salt and pepper. Sauce can be stored in an airtight container in refrigerator for up to 1 week.

2. Cook the pasta: Bring salted water to a boil in a Dutch oven. Add pasta and cook until *al dente*.

3. Serve: Drain pasta, add to sauce and stir.

✱ This pasta dish can be stored in an airtight container in refrigerator for up to 3 days.

PASTA IN CREAMY ZUCCHINI-LEMON SAUCE

SERVES 4-6

A velvety sauce with the aroma and flavor of lemon combined with zucchini and whole-wheat pasta.

INGREDIENTS

For the sauce:
2 tablespoons butter
4 medium zucchini, cut into 1½ inch thick slices (2 colors are recommended)
1½ cups half and half
Zest of 1 lemon
2 tablespoons lemon juice
Salt and ground black pepper, to taste

1 pound whole-wheat pasta

PREPARATION

1. Prepare the sauce: Add 1 tablespoon of butter and zucchini to a large skillet over medium-high heat. Sauté for 8-10 minutes, until golden brown. Repeat with remaining butter and zucchini. Add half and half, lemon zest, lemon juice, salt and pepper, stir and bring to a boil. Cook for 2 minutes, until the sauce is thick.

2. Cook the pasta: Bring salted water to a boil in a Dutch oven. Add pasta and cook until *al dente*.

3. Serve: Drain pasta, add to sauce and stir.

✱ This pasta dish can be stored in an airtight container in refrigerator for up to 3 days. Reheat in microwave.

TOMATO-SPINACH LASAGNA

MAKES A 9X13-INCH PAN

A classic Italian dish. This version features a tomato, spinach, ricotta and mozzarella filling.

PREPARATION

1. Prepare the spinach: Heat a large saucepan over medium heat. Add olive oil and spinach and cook for 2 minutes, stirring occasionally, just until the spinach starts to wilt. (The spinach continues to wilt after it is taken off the heat.) Drain. Press the spinach firmly by hand to remove any excess liquid.

2. Prepare the sauce: Heat a large skillet over medium heat, add olive oil, onion and garlic and sauté for 5 minutes, stirring occasionally, until the onion and garlic are tender. Add wine and sugar, bring to a boil and cook, until the wine is completely reduced. Add crushed tomatoes, salt and pepper, stir and bring to a boil. Taste and adjust seasoning with salt and pepper. Cool.

INGREDIENTS

For the spinach:
1 tablespoon olive oil
10 oz. fresh spinach

For the sauce:
$1/4$ cup olive oil
1 medium onion, finely chopped
4 garlic cloves, finely chopped
$1/3$ cup dry white wine
1 teaspoon sugar
28 oz. canned crushed tomatoes

Salt and ground black pepper, to taste

18 no boil lasagna noodles

For the filling:
1 pound part-skim ricotta cheese
12 oz. mozzarella cheese, shredded

3. Assemble the lasagna: Preheat oven to 350°F and grease a 9x13-inch pan. Arrange 6 overlapping lasagna noodles in the pan, cut noodles to fit pan, if necessary. Add a third of the sauce, scatter a third of the cooked spinach, a third of the ricotta and a third of the mozzarella. Place a second layer of lasagna noodles, then the sauce, cooked spinach, ricotta and mozzarella. Repeat the process for a third layer.

4. Bake for 40-50 minutes, until golden. Let the lasagna stand for 10 minutes and then slice.

✱ Lasagna can be stored in an airtight container in refrigerator for up to 3 days. Reheat in a preheated oven at 350°F.

¤ *Tomato-Spinach Lasagna*

TOMATO, GARLIC & THYME RISOTTO

SERVES 4

This risotto doesn't contain any fresh tomatoes. Instead, it relies on tomato juice (instead of vegetable stock) and sun-dried tomatoes to supply its rich and uniquely tomato flavor.

INGREDIENTS

2 cups tomato juice
4 cups water
4 tablespoons butter
1 medium onion, finely diced
8 garlic cloves, coarsely chopped
2 sprigs thyme, leaves only
1 1/2 cups arborio rice
Salt and ground black pepper, to taste
1/3 cup sun-dried tomatoes, sliced
   into strips
1/2 cup dry white wine

For serving:
Grated Parmesan cheese, to taste

PREPARATION

1. Heat tomato juice and water in a large saucepan and bring to a boil. Reduce heat and keep at low boil during entire risotto cooking process.

2. Melt butter in a large skillet over medium-low heat. Add onion, garlic and thyme leaves and sauté for 5 minutes, stirring occasionally, until the onion and garlic are tender.

3. Add rice, salt and pepper and sauté for 2 minutes, stirring continuously, until the rice is hot and coated in butter. Add sun-dried tomatoes and wine and cook for 2 minutes, stirring continuously, until the wine reduces.

4. Add a ladleful of the tomato stock. Cook, stirring continuously, until the liquid is absorbed. Continue adding stock, 1 ladleful at a time for 20 minutes, until rice is cooked *al dente*. (It is possible that the rice will be ready before all the stock has been used; make sure to taste the rice after 20 minutes of cooking.) Taste and adjust seasoning with salt and pepper. Remove from heat, sprinkle with Parmesan and serve immediately.

＊ Risotto can be stored in an airtight container in refrigerator for up to 3 days. Reheat in microwave.

BEET RISOTTO

SERVES 4

The beet colors the rice a deep crimson and lends it a sweet earthy flavor.

INGREDIENTS

6 cups vegetable stock
3 tablespoons butter
1 medium onion, finely diced
2 garlic cloves, coarsely chopped
1 1/2 cups arborio rice
Salt and ground black pepper, to taste
1/2 cup dry white wine
2 medium beets, cooked, peeled
   and cut into 1/4-inch cubes

For serving:
Grated Parmesan cheese, to taste
1/4 cup chives, finely chopped

PREPARATION

1. Heat the stock, keeping it at a low boil during entire risotto cooking process.

2. Melt butter in a large saucepan over medium heat. Add onion and garlic and cook for 5 minutes, stirring occasionally, until the onion and garlic are tender.

3. Add rice, salt and pepper and sauté for 2 minutes, stirring continuously, until the rice is hot and coated in butter. Add wine and cook for 2 minutes, stirring continuously, until the wine reduces.

4. Add cubes of beet and a ladleful of stock. Cook, stirring continuously, until the liquid is absorbed. Continue adding stock, 1 ladleful at a time, for 20 minutes until rice is *al dente*. Taste and adjust seasoning with salt and pepper. Remove from heat, sprinkle with Parmesan and chives and serve immediately.

✱ Risotto can be stored in an airtight container in refrigerator for up to 3 days. Reheat in microwave.

PEA
&
MINT
RISOTTO

SERVES 4

The ideal flavor combination
of fresh green peas and mint
works beautifully in this risotto.

INGREDIENTS

6 cups vegetable stock
3 tablespoons butter
1 medium onion, finely diced
2 garlic cloves, coarsely chopped
1$^1/_2$ cups arborio rice
Salt and ground black pepper, to taste
$^1/_2$ cup dry white wine
$^1/_2$ cup half and half
2 cups shelled fresh green peas
$^1/_2$ cup mint, coarsely chopped

For serving:
Grated Parmesan cheese, to taste

PREPARATION

1. Heat the stock, keeping it at a low boil during entire risotto cooking process.

2. Melt butter in a large saucepan over medium heat. Add onion and garlic and sauté for 5 minutes, stirring occasionally, until the onion and garlic are tender.

3. Add rice, salt and pepper and sauté for 2 minutes, stirring continuously, until the rice is hot and coated in butter. Add wine and cook for 2 minutes, stirring continuously, until the wine reduces.

4. Add a ladleful of stock and cook, stirring continuously, until the liquid is absorbed. Continue adding stock, 1 ladleful at a time, for 20 minutes until rice is almost cooked.

5. Add half and half, peas and mint, stir and bring to a boil. Cook until the rice is *al dente*. Taste and adjust seasoning with salt and pepper. Remove from heat, sprinkle with Parmesan and serve immediately.

✱ Risotto can be stored in an airtight container in refrigerator for up to 3 days. Reheat in microwave.

¤ *Pea & Mint Risotto*

¤ *Rice Pilaf with Carrots, Spinach & Raisins*

RICE PILAF WITH CARROTS, SPINACH & RAISINS

SERVES 4

This is a special-occasion rice dish that is equally suited as a side dish or a vegetarian main by itself.

INGREDIENTS

3 tablespoons olive oil
1 medium onion, finely chopped
2 medium carrots, peeled and coarsely grated
2 cups basmati rice
3 cups boiling water
$1/2$ cup golden raisins
Salt and ground black pepper, to taste
2 cups spinach, coarsely chopped

PREPARATION

1. Heat a large saucepan over medium heat, add olive oil, onion and carrots and sauté for 5-7 minutes, stirring occasionally, until the carrots and onion are tender.

2. Add rice and sauté for another minute, stirring continuously, until the rice is hot and coated in oil. Add boiling water, raisins, salt and pepper, stir and bring to a boil. Reduce heat, cover and cook for 20 minutes, until the rice is cooked.

3. Remove from heat. Add spinach, stir and cover for 10 minutes. Taste and adjust seasoning with salt and pepper.

✳ This rice pilaf can be stored in an airtight container in refrigerator for up to 3 days. Reheat in microwave.

QUINOA WITH MUSHROOMS

SERVES 6

The combination of dried and fresh mushrooms lends the quinoa a complex, earthy flavor.

INGREDIENTS

3 tablespoons olive oil
1 large onion, diced
7 oz. dried porcini mushrooms,
    soaked in a cup of boiling water
10 oz. button mushrooms, sliced
    $1/4$-inch thick
Zest of 1 lemon
3 cups quinoa
$3^1/_2$ cups boiling water
Salt and ground black pepper, to taste

For serving:
$1/_3$ cup lemon juice
2 green onions (white & green part),
    thinly sliced

PREPARATION

1. Heat a large saucepan over medium heat, add olive oil and onion and cook for 5 minutes, stirring continuously, until the onion is tender.

2. Drain and slice porcini mushrooms, reserving soaking liquid. Add all mushrooms and lemon zest to onion. Sauté for 2 minutes, stirring continuously.

3. Add quinoa, the soaking liquid from the porcini mushrooms, water, salt and pepper and bring to a boil.

4. Reduce heat, cover and cook for 20-25 minutes, until the quinoa is tender. Add lemon juice and green onion, stir, taste and adjust seasoning with salt and pepper.

✱ This quinoa dish can be stored in an airtight container in refrigerator for up to 3 days. Reheat in microwave.

PEARL BARLEY WITH BROCCOLINI

SERVES 4-6

Broccolini is a slimmer version of broccoli, created by crossing it with Chinese broccoli.
It's the perfect summer vegetable. Broccolini, with its smaller florets and longer, thinner stalks, is reminiscent of asparagus. Here it is used in a homestyle dish with pearl barley.

INGREDIENTS

3 tablespoons olive oil
1 medium onion, coarsely chopped
2 cups pearl barley, rinsed and drained well
10 oz. broccolini, cut into $1/2$-inch pieces
3 cups water
Salt and ground black pepper, to taste

PREPARATION

1. Heat a large saucepan over medium heat, add olive oil and onion and cook for 5 minutes, until the onion is tender. Add pearl barley and sauté for 2 minutes, stirring continuously, until the barley is hot and coated in oil.

2. Add broccolini, water, salt and pepper and bring to a boil.

3. Remove from heat. Cover and cook for 20–25 minutes, until the barley is soft but still holds its shape. Taste and adjust seasoning with salt and pepper.

✳ This dish can be stored in an airtight container in refrigerator for up to 3 days. Reheat in microwave.

¤ *Peppers Stuffed with Red Rice*

PEPPERS STUFFED WITH RED RICE

SERVES 8

Sun-dried tomato spread adds great flavor to the cooking liquid.

INGREDIENTS

8 medium peppers, stemmed and seeded for stuffing

For the cooking liquid:
$4^{1}/_{4}$ cups boiling water
$^{1}/_{3}$ cup sun-dried tomato spread
Salt and ground black pepper, to taste

For filling:
$^{1}/_{4}$ cup olive oil
1 large onion, finely diced
4 garlic cloves, coarsely chopped
2 cups red rice, rinsed and drained (or substitute brown rice)
$1^{1}/_{2}$ teaspoons sweet paprika
Salt and ground black pepper, to taste
1 cup mixed herbs (parsley, cilantro and mint), finely chopped

PREPARATION

1. Prepare the cooking liquid: Stir boiling water, sun-dried tomato spread, salt and pepper in a wide pot. Set aside.

2. Prepare the filling: Add $1^{1}/_{2}$ tablespoons of olive oil, onion and garlic to a large saucepan over medium heat. Sauté for 5 minutes, stirring continuously, until the onion and garlic are softened. Add rice, paprika, salt and pepper and sauté for 2 minutes, stirring continuously. (Take care not to burn paprika, as it scorches easily.) Add half the quantity of cooking liquid to the rice (set aside the remaining liquid for cooking the stuffed peppers) and bring to a boil. Cover with lid, reduce heat and cook for 20-25 minutes, until the rice has absorbed all the liquid. Add herbs and stir. Taste and adjust seasoning with salt and pepper.

3. Stuff peppers with rice until they are $^{3}/_{4}$ full, place them closely together in the saucepan with the remaining cooking liquid and bring to a boil.

4. Reduce heat, cover and cook for 50-60 minutes, until the rice is cooked.

5. Turn off heat, cover with lid and allow it to rest for 10 minutes.

✳ This dish can be stored in an airtight container in refrigerator for up to 3 days. Reheat in microwave.

LENTIL, TOMATO & PINE NUT PASTA SALAD

SERVES 6-8

This cold pasta salad with lentils, yellow and red cherry tomatoes, pine nuts and chives is a complete meal all on its own.

2 cups green lentils

1 pound whole-wheat pasta

2 tablespoons olive oil

1 1/4 pounds yellow and red cherry tomatoes, quartered

1/2 cup toasted pine nuts

1/3 cup chives, finely chopped

For the dressing:

1/4 cup olive oil

2 tablespoons white wine vinegar

2 tablespoons lemon juice

4 anchovy filets, finely chopped (optional)

2 garlic cloves, crushed

1 teaspoon smooth Dijon mustard

Salt and ground black pepper, to taste

PREPARATION

1. Cook lentils in a large saucepan of unsalted boiling water for 25-35 minutes, until tender. Drain well.

2. Bring a Dutch oven of salted water to a boil. Add pasta and cook until *al dente*. Drain well. Pour 2 tablespoons of olive oil over pasta and stir to prevent pasta from sticking together. Cool thoroughly.

3. Transfer pasta to a large bowl and add lentils, tomatoes, pine nuts and chives. Mix dressing ingredients well. Pour dressing over salad and stir. Taste and adjust seasoning with salt and pepper.

✱ The pasta salad can be stored in an airtight container in refrigerator for up to 3 days.

¤ *Lentil, Tomato & Pine Nut Pasta Salad*

¤ *Rice Pilaf with Mushrooms & Sweet Potato*

RICE PILAF WITH MUSHROOMS & SWEET POTATO

SERVES 4

Pilaf, with its origins in Persia, is a hot rice dish that comes in endless versions. This version is vegetarian, using sweet potato and mushrooms without the traditional beef or chicken.

INGREDIENTS

2 tablespoons olive oil
1 medium onion, finely chopped
2 garlic cloves, chopped
1 small sweet potato, cut into $1/4$-inch cubes
7 oz. mushrooms, halved and cut into $1/4$-inch thick slices
2 cups basmati rice
4 cups boiling water
Salt and ground black pepper, to taste

PREPARATION

1. Add olive oil, onion and garlic to a large saucepan over medium heat. Sauté for 5 minutes, stirring continuously, until the onion and garlic are softened. Add potato, mushrooms and rice and sauté for 2 minutes, stirring continuously.

2. Add boiling water, salt and black pepper, stir and bring to a boil. Reduce heat, cover and cook for 20 minutes, until the rice is cooked. Remove from heat, stir and let stand covered for 10 minutes. Taste and adjust seasoning with salt and pepper.

* The pilaf can be stored in an airtight container in refrigerator for up to 3 days. Reheat in microwave.

COUSCOUS WITH STIR-FRIED VEGETABLES

SERVES 6-8

Instead of the traditional Moroccan vegetable soup, this couscous is served with an assortment of vegetables stir-fried in olive oil.

INGREDIENTS

12 oz. quick-cooking whole-wheat couscous
3 tablespoons olive oil
1 medium sweet potato, cut into $1/2$-inch cubes
1 small eggplant, cut into $1/2$-inch cubes
1 medium onion, finely chopped
1 medium zucchini, cut into $1/2$-inch cubes
1 medium red pepper, cut into $1/2$-inch cubes
Salt and ground black pepper, to taste
2 tablespoons lemon juice
1 tablespoon balsamic vinegar
$1/3$ cup parsley, finely chopped

PREPARATION

1. Prepare couscous according to package instructions and transfer to a large bowl. Fluff with a fork to separate grains.

2. Heat olive oil in a wok or large, deep skillet over medium heat. Add sweet potato and eggplant and sauté, stirring occasionally, until vegetables start to brown. Add onion, zucchini, red pepper, salt and pepper and stir-fry for 5 minutes, until vegetables are tender. Add couscous, lemon juice, balsamic vinegar and parsley and stir.

3. Taste and adjust seasoning with salt and pepper.

✱ The couscous and vegetables can be stored in an airtight container in refrigerator for up to 3 days. Reheat in microwave.

ASIAN-STYLE GLASS NOODLE SALAD

SERVES 6

Glass or cellophane noodles are made from bean flour, are neutral in taste and readily absorb seasoning, especially the intense flavors of the Asian kitchen.

INGREDIENTS

7 oz. glass noodles (bean thread), soaked in hot water for 10 minutes
2 medium carrots, peeled and julienned
1 cup bean sprouts
1/4 medium red cabbage, cut into thin strips
4 green onions, thinly sliced
1/2 cup cilantro, finely chopped
1/4 cup mint leaves
1/4 cup basil leaves
1/2 cup salted peanuts, coarsely chopped

For the dressing:
1/4 cup lime (or lemon) juice
1/4 cup fish sauce
1/4 cup soy sauce
1/4 cup water
2 tablespoons rice vinegar
2 tablespoons sugar
2 garlic cloves, crushed
1 shallot, peeled and diced
2 teaspoons fresh ginger, finely chopped
1 chili pepper, thinly sliced into rings (optional)

PREPARATION

1. Mix dressing ingredients in a large bowl and wait until the sugar dissolves.

2. Drain noodles well and transfer to the bowl with the dressing. Add carrots, sprouts, red cabbage, green onion and cilantro and stir. Toss with mint, basil and peanuts.

* The noodle salad can be stored in an airtight container in refrigerator for up to 2 days.

MEAT & FISH

NOODLES WITH CHICKEN & VEGETABLES

SERVES 4-6

The trick to making noodle stir-fries and other Asian dishes is to get all the ingredients ready in advance — then all that's left to do is stir-fry in a hot pan and serve.

INGREDIENTS

7 oz. noodles (any Asian noodles work, but whole-wheat are healthier)

1 head broccoli, cut into small florets

2 tablespoons canola oil

10 oz. boneless skinless chicken breast, cut into 1-inch strips

1 large red pepper, cut into thin strips

1 large carrot, peeled and cut into thin sticks

1 cup cabbage, cut into thin strips

2 garlic cloves, coarsely chopped

3 tablespoons soy sauce

3 tablespoons sweet chili sauce

1 tablespoon honey

1 teaspoon sesame oil

1 tablespoon sesame seeds

Salt and ground black pepper, to taste

PREPARATION

1. Cook noodles according to package instructions.

2. Cook broccoli in salted boiling water, until crisp-tender. Drain well.

3. Heat a wok or large frying pan over high heat, add canola oil and chicken strips and stir-fry for 2 minutes, until the chicken is cooked through.

4. Remove chicken to plate with a slotted spoon.

5. Add red pepper, carrot, cabbage and garlic and stir-fry for 2-3 minutes, until vegetables start to soften. Add remaining ingredients, including chicken, broccoli and noodles and stir-fry for about 2 minutes to combine flavors.

✳ The noodles can be stored in an airtight container in refrigerator for up to 2 days. Reheat in microwave.

¤ *Noodles with Chicken & Vegetables*

CHICKEN SALAD WITH CABBAGE & PEAS

SERVES 4

This salad is a wonderful way to enjoy yesterday's leftover chicken.

INGREDIENTS

1 cup shelled fresh green peas
1lb roasted or cooked chicken breast, sliced into strips
2 cups cabbage, cut into thin strips
1/4 cup cilantro, finely chopped

1 tablespoon lemon juice
1 teaspoon honey
1 teaspoon mustard
Salt and ground black pepper, to taste

For the dressing:
3 tablespoons canola oil
4 teaspoons mayonnaise
1 tablespoon white wine vinegar

PREPARATION

1. Cook peas for 3-4 minutes in salted boiling water, until crisp-tender. Drain well and transfer to a bowl. Add chicken, cabbage and cilantro.

2. Mix dressing ingredients well, add to salad and toss. Taste and adjust seasoning with salt and pepper.

✳ This salad can be stored in an airtight container in refrigerator for up to 2 days.

CHICKEN SCALLOPINI IN COCONUT MILK WITH SWEET POTATO

SERVES 2-4

Italian scallopini, made with paper-thin slices of veal and cream, is given a modern, casual makeover with chicken and coconut milk.

INGREDIENTS

2 boneless skinless chicken breasts, split to make 4 pieces
Salt and ground black pepper, to taste
1/4 cup flour for coating chicken
3 tablespoons canola oil
1 small sweet potato, peeled and cut into 1/2-inch cubes
1 garlic clove, crushed
1 teaspoon fresh ginger, grated

1 1/2 cups coconut milk
1/2 teaspoon curry powder
Salt and ground black pepper, to taste

For serving:
1/2 cup cilantro, coarsely chopped

PREPARATION

1. Remove the chicken from the refrigerator about 30 minutes before cooking.

2. Season chicken with salt and pepper and dust with a thin, even layer of flour. Heat a large skillet over medium heat, add canola oil and chicken breasts and cook for 2-3 minutes each side, until lightly browned. Remove to a plate.

3. Add cubes of sweet potato to skillet and stir-fry for 4-6 minutes, until lightly browned. Add garlic and ginger and sauté, stirring continuously, for another minute. Add coconut milk, curry, salt and pepper, stir and bring to a boil.

4. Return chicken to pan and skillet for 20 minutes, uncovered, until the sauce thickens and the chicken is cooked through. Taste and adjust seasoning with salt and pepper.

5. Sprinkle with chopped cilantro and serve.

* This chicken dish can be stored in an airtight container in refrigerator for up to 2 days. Reheat in microwave.

CHICKEN BREASTS IN PEPPERS & OLIVES

SERVES 4

When chicken is cooked in a pan with sauce it turns out especially juicy. Serve this dish with fresh bread for soaking up the sauce.

INGREDIENTS

2 boneless chicken breasts, skin on, split to make 4 pieces
$1/4$ cup olive oil
1 medium onion, halved and cut into $1/4$-inch thick slices
2 large peppers (2 colors recommended), cut into $1/2$-inch thick strips
$1/3$ cup dry white wine
$1/3$ cup water
1 tablespoon tomato paste
16 Kalamata olives, pitted
2 sprigs thyme, leaves only
Salt and ground black pepper, to taste

PREPARATION

1. Remove the chicken from the refrigerator about 45 minutes before cooking.

2. Heat a large saucepan over medium heat, add olive oil, then chicken and cook for 3-4 minutes per side, until lightly browned.

3. Remove chicken to a plate, add onions and peppers to saucepan and sauté for about 5 minutes, stirring occasionally, until lightly browned. Return chicken to saucepan, add wine, water, tomato paste, olives, thyme, salt and pepper, stir and bring to a boil.

4. Reduce heat, cover and cook for 10 minutes, until the chicken is cooked through. Taste and adjust seasoning with salt and pepper.

✱ The chicken dish can be stored in an airtight container in refrigerator for up to 2 days. Reheat in microwave.

¤ *Roasted Chicken with Moroccan-Style Sweet Potatoes*

ROASTED CHICKEN WITH MOROCCAN-STYLE SWEET POTATOES

SERVES 4-6

This juicy chicken is coated in an aromatic herb paste. Finish roasting breast side down to prevent the chicken from drying out.

1 whole chicken, about 4 to 4$\frac{1}{2}$ pounds
3 medium sweet potatoes, peeled and cut into 2-inch cubes
$\frac{1}{2}$ cup water

For the sauce:
2 teaspoons sweet paprika
$\frac{1}{2}$ teaspoon hot paprika
$\frac{1}{2}$ teaspoon cumin
$\frac{1}{2}$ teaspoon ground coriander
$\frac{1}{2}$ teaspoon cinnamon
$\frac{1}{4}$ cup olive oil
3 tablespoons lemon juice
Salt, to taste

PREPARATION

1. Remove chicken from refrigerator about an hour before cooking.

2. Preheat oven to 400°F and line a baking pan with parchment paper. Mix sauce ingredients in a small bowl, place sweet potatoes in the baking pan, pour water and a third of the sauce over them and mix well.

3. Tie chicken legs together with string. Place chicken over sweet potatoes, breast side up. Cover chicken with remaining sauce.

4. Bake for 40 minutes, turn chicken over and bake for another 40 minutes, until the chicken is golden brown and fully cooked and the sweet potatoes are tender.

✱ This chicken dish can be stored in an airtight container in refrigerator for up to 2 days. Reheat in a preheated 350°F oven.

BEEF, ARUGULA & RADISH SALAD

SERVES 4

A colorful, palate-pleasing summer salad.

INGREDIENTS

$1\frac{1}{4}$ pounds sirloin
2 tablespoons olive oil
6 cups arugula
4 radishes, thinly sliced
$\frac{1}{2}$ small red onion, thinly sliced

For the dressing:
2 tablespoons olive oil
1 tablespoon balsamic vinegar
1 tablespoon lemon juice
1 shallot, finely chopped
Salt and ground black pepper, to taste

PREPARATION

1. Remove meat from refrigerator about 45 minutes before cooking.

2. Preheat oven to 400°F and line a baking pan with parchment paper.

3. Coat the meat in olive oil and place in baking pan. Bake for 20 minutes for medium doneness. Cool for 10 minutes, slice meat into $\frac{1}{2}$-inch strips and transfer to a bowl. Add arugula, radish and onion.

4. Mix dressing ingredients well, pour over salad and toss. Taste and adjust seasoning with salt and pepper.

✱ The salad can be stored in an airtight container in refrigerator for up to 2 days.

STIR-FRIED BEEF WITH CABBAGE & TOMATOES

SERVES 4

A lighter meat dish that is quick to prepare.

INGREDIENTS

3/4 pound sirloin, thinly sliced
2 tablespoons canola oil
Half of a medium green cabbage, thinly sliced
2 medium tomatoes, cut into 1-inch cubes
2 tablespoons soy sauce
2 tablespoons sweet chili sauce
Salt and ground black pepper, to taste

PREPARATION

1. Remove meat from refrigerator about 30 minutes before cooking.

2. Heat oil in wok over high heat. Add meat and stir-fry for a minute or two, just until the meat changes color. Transfer meat to a plate.

3. Add cabbage, tomatoes, soy sauce, chili sauce and a small amount of salt and pepper to wok and stir-fry for about 2 minutes, until the vegetables start to soften.

4. Return meat to wok and stir-fry for a minute to integrate flavors. Taste and adjust seasoning with salt and pepper.

✱ This stir-fried dish can be stored in an airtight container in refrigerator for up to 2 days. Reheat in microwave.

SIRLOIN SKEWERS WITH PEPPERS & ONIONS

SERVES 4

So easy, so tasty: oven-roasted skewers of beef, peppers and onions.

INGREDIENTS

$1^1/_2$ pounds sirloin, cut into $^1/_2$-inch cubes
1 large bell pepper, cut into $1^1/_2$-inch cubes
1 medium onion, peeled and cut into quarters
3 tablespoons olive oil
4 teaspoons mustard
Salt and ground black pepper, to taste

PREPARATION

1. Remove meat from refrigerator about 60 minutes before cooking.

2. Preheat oven to 400°F and line a baking pan with parchment paper. Mix olive oil, mustard, salt and pepper.

3. Add cubes of meat, pepper and onion and mix well. Spear 2 cubes of meat, 2 pepper cubes and 2 onion cubes, alternating, onto each skewer and place in baking pan.

4. Bake for 10 minutes until cooked.

✳ The skewers can be stored in an airtight container in refrigerator for up to 2 days.

¤ *Sirloin Skewers with Peppers & Onions*

ASIAN-STYLE BEEF SALAD

SERVES 4

Cold beef is an excellent match for Asian flavors like fish sauce and soy sauce.

INGREDIENTS

$1^1/_4$ pounds sirloin
2 tablespoons olive oil
10 oz. snow peas
2 medium cucumbers, sliced in half lengthwise
1 small red onion, halved and thinly sliced
$^1/_3$ cup basil

For the dressing:
2 tablespoons fish sauce
2 tablespoons soy sauce
2 tablespoons canola oil
2 teaspoons lemon juice
1 tablespoon mirin
1 tablespoon rice vinegar
1 shallot, finely chopped

PREPARATION

1. Remove meat from refrigerator about 45 minutes before cooking.

2. Preheat oven to 400°F and line a baking pan with parchment paper. Coat the meat in olive oil and place in baking pan.

3. Bake for 20 minutes for medium doneness. Cool for 10 minutes.

4. Cook snow peas for 2-3 minutes in salted boiling water, until crisp-tender. Seed the halved cucumbers and slice into $^1/_4$-inch pieces. Slice meat into $^1/_2$-inch strips and transfer to a bowl. Add snow peas, cucumber, onion and basil.

5. Mix dressing ingredients well, pour over salad and toss. Taste and adjust seasoning with salt and pepper.

✱ The salad can be stored in an airtight container in refrigerator for up to 2 days.

¤ *Asian-Style Beef Salad*

SHEPHERD'S PIE WITH CARROTS & PEAS

MAKES A 12 X 8-INCH DISH

This well-known British dish gets a fresh pick-me-up with carrots and peas.

INGREDIENTS

For the mashed potatoes:
6 medium potatoes, peeled and cut into 2-inch cubes
1 tablespoon coarse sea salt
2 tablespoons butter
Pinch of freshly ground nutmeg
Salt and ground black pepper, to taste

For the filling:
$1/4$ cup olive oil
2 medium onions, coarsely chopped
2 medium carrots, cut into $1/4$-inch cubes
$1 1/4$ pounds ground beef
1 tablespoon flour
$1/2$ cup dry red wine
1 cup shelled fresh green peas
2 sprigs thyme, leaves only
Salt and ground black pepper, to taste

PREPARATION

1. Preheat oven to 400°F. Place potato cubes in a large saucepan, fill with enough water to cover the potatoes by at least an inch, add the coarse sea salt and bring to a boil. Reduce heat and cook for 25 minutes, until the potatoes are tender.

2. In the meantime prepare the filling: Heat a large skillet over medium heat. Add olive oil, onions and carrots and cook for about 10 minutes, until the onions and carrots are tender. Add meat and cook while breaking up the meat, until the beef turns brown. Add flour, wine, peas, thyme, salt and pepper, stir and bring to a boil.

3. Cook uncovered for about 5 minutes, until the liquids reduce and thicken. Taste and adjust seasoning with salt and pepper. Transfer the meat mixture to a baking dish.

4. Drain the potatoes, mash them, add butter, nutmeg, salt and pepper and stir. Taste and adjust seasoning with salt and pepper. Top the meat mixture with mashed potatoes. (The best technique is to place potatoes along the edges of the dish and spread towards the center.) Bake for 30 minutes, until golden brown.

✱ The Shepherd's pie can be stored in an airtight container in refrigerator for up to 2 days. Reheat in microwave.

¤ *Shepherd's Pie with Carrots & Peas*

SIRLOIN STEAK IN MUSHROOM & WINE SAUCE

SERVES 4

This is not a dish to prepare in advance, but one that is made in a minute and served immediately, as soon as the steak is done.

INGREDIENTS

4 sirloin steaks, about 1-inch thick
1 tablespoon olive oil
Salt and ground black pepper, to taste

For the sauce:
2 tablespoons olive oil
1 pound mushrooms (best to use two varieties), cut into $1/4$-inch slices
$1/3$ cup dry red wine
1 sprig thyme, leaves only
Salt and ground black pepper, to taste
3 tablespoons butter

PREPARATION

1. Remove steaks from refrigerator about 45 minutes before cooking.

2. Prepare the sauce: Heat a large saucepan over high heat. Add olive oil and mushrooms and sauté for about 5 minutes, stirring occasionally, until golden brown. Add wine, thyme, salt and pepper and bring to a boil. Cook for 5 minutes, until the wine reduces. Add butter and stir until melted. Taste and adjust seasoning with salt and pepper. Remove from heat and cover to keep warm.

3. Prepare the steaks: Heat a cast iron skillet (regular or grill) over high heat. Coat the meat in olive oil and season with salt and pepper. Place steak on hot pan and sauté for 3 minutes per side, until golden brown.

4. Reduce heat and continue cooking for an additional 1 minute per side for medium doneness. Serve steak with the warm sauce.

✱ This steak dish can be stored in an airtight container in refrigerator for up to 2 days. Reheat in microwave.

SHRIMP, AVOCADO & SPROUT SALAD

SERVES 6

The trick to this salad is to quickly cook the shrimp and then immediately coat them in lemon juice and olive oil. This way, the shrimp absorbs all that flavorful liquid, becoming especially juicy.

INGREDIENTS

1$\frac{1}{2}$ pounds fresh peeled and deveined shrimp, with tails on
3 tablespoons lemon juice
2 tablespoons olive oil
1 large avocado, peeled and cut into 1-inch cubes
1 cup sunflower sprouts
Salt and ground black pepper, to taste

PREPARATION

1. Bring a large saucepan of salted water to a boil. Cook shrimp for about 2 minutes, until just pink.

2. Drain well and transfer to a bowl. Immediately add lemon juice and olive oil and mix. Cool for 10 minutes.

3. Add avocado, sprouts, salt and black pepper and stir. Taste and adjust seasoning with salt and pepper.

＊ The salad can be stored in an airtight container in refrigerator for up to 2 days.

OSSO BUCO WITH FENNEL & TOMATOES

SERVES 4-6

In this luxurious dish, the fennel soaks up all the divine flavor of the sauce and the meat.

INGREDIENTS

6 slices of veal shank
   (or 4 large slices), about 1-inch thick
   (ask your butcher to do this for you)
$1/3$ cup flour for coating veal
$1/4$ cup + 2 tablespoons olive oil
1 large onion, finely chopped
2 celery stalks, cut into $1/2$-inch cubes
2 medium carrots, peeled and cut
   into $1/2$ -inch cubes

2 cups dry red wine
$1^1/_2$ cups water
28 oz. canned crushed tomatoes
3 bay leaves
Salt and ground black pepper, to taste
2 fennel bulbs, quartered

For serving:
Thyme sprigs, coarsely
   chopped

PREPARATION

1. Remove veal from refrigerator about 60 minutes before cooking.

2. Lightly flour the meat, heat a Dutch oven over medium heat, add $1/4$ cup of olive oil and sauté for 2-3 minutes per side, until lightly browned. Transfer meat to a plate. Add 2 remaining tablespoons of olive oil to Dutch oven, then add onion, celery and carrot and sauté for 10 minutes, stirring occasionally, until the vegetables are tender. Pour in wine and water, add tomatoes, bay leaves, salt and pepper and stir.

3. Place meat in Dutch oven (make sure all the meat is fully immersed in liquid) and bring to a boil.

4. Reduce heat, cover Dutch oven with lid and cook for 2 hours. Add fennel and bring to a boil. Reduce heat, cover with lid and cook for another half an hour, until the meat and fennel are tender. Taste and adjust seasoning with salt and pepper.

5. Sprinkle with chopped thyme and serve.

✳ The Osso Buco can be stored in an airtight container in refrigerator for up to 3 days. Reheat in microwave or in a Dutch oven on the stove.

CHICKEN SCALLOPINI WITH ZUCCHINI, LEMON & CAPERS

SERVES 2-4

Chicken breast and cubes of zucchini pair well with the tart flavors of lemon and capers.

INGREDIENTS

2 boneless skinless chicken breasts, split to make 4 pieces
Salt and ground black pepper, to taste
$1/3$ cup flour for coating chicken
2 tablespoons olive oil
2 medium zucchini, cut into $1/2$-inch cubes
$1/2$ lemon, cut into $1/4$-inch slices
$1/4$ cup lemon juice
$1/4$ cup water
2 tablespoons large capers
$1/2$ teaspoon sugar
Salt and ground black pepper, to taste

PREPARATION

1. Remove chicken from refrigerator 30 minutes prior to cooking.

2. Season chicken with salt and black pepper and dust with flour, shaking off excess to achieve a thin, uniform layer of flour on each piece of chicken.

3. Heat a large skillet over medium heat, add olive oil and chicken and cook for 2-3 minutes on each side, until golden. Transfer to a plate.

4. Add cubes of zucchini and stir-fry for 3-5 minutes, until zucchini browns. Add lemon slices, lemon juice, water, capers, sugar, salt and black pepper, stir and bring to a boil. Return chicken to pan and cook for 20 minutes, uncovered, until the sauce thickens and the chicken is cooked through. Taste and adjust seasoning with salt and pepper.

＊ The scallopini can be stored in an airtight container in refrigerator for up to 2 days. Reheat in microwave.

¤ *Chicken Scallopini with Zucchini, Lemon & Capers*

STIR-FRIED SHRIMP WITH WHITE BEANS & SPINACH

SERVES 4

It takes a single skillet to make this satisfying meal.

INGREDIENTS

3 tablespoons butter
2 large garlic cloves, coarsely chopped
$1/2$ chili pepper, thinly sliced into rings (optional)
$1^1/4$ pounds fresh peeled and deveined shrimp, with tails on
3 cups cooked white beans
$1/3$ cup dry white wine
3 cups fresh spinach, coarsely chopped
$1/4$ cup chives, finely chopped
Salt and ground black pepper, to taste

PREPARATION

1. Melt butter in a large skillet over medium heat.

2. Add garlic, chili and shrimp and sauté for about 1 minute, stirring continuously, just until the shrimp starts changing color. Add beans and white wine and bring to a boil. Cook uncovered over high heat for about 2 minutes, until the wine reduces.

3. Add spinach, chives, salt and pepper, stir and bring to a boil again. Taste and adjust seasoning with salt and pepper.

* This dish can be stored in an airtight container in refrigerator for up to 2 days. Reheat in microwave.

¤ *Stir-Fried Shrimp with White Beans & Spinach*

TUNA WITH PEPPER CHUTNEY

SERVES 4

Tuna is at its best when seared for just a couple of minutes on each side, leaving it cool and deep red in the center.

INGREDIENTS

1 pound fresh tuna
1 tablespoon olive oil

For the chutney:
3 large red peppers, cut into $^1/_2$-inch cubes
2 large garlic cloves, coarsely chopped
$^1/_2$ green pepper, finely chopped (optional)
1 inch fresh ginger, peeled and julienned
$^1/_4$ cup vinegar
$^1/_4$ cup light brown sugar

PREPARATION

1. Remove fish from refrigerator about 20 minutes before cooking.

2. Prepare the chutney: Cook all chutney ingredients in a small saucepan over medium heat, until the sugar melts. Bring to a boil and cook uncovered over medium-low heat for about half an hour, stirring occasionally, until liquids are cooked down and the peppers are tender. Cool thoroughly.

3. Prepare the fish: Spread olive oil over tuna and sear in a hot skillet for 2-3 minutes per side.

4. Serve: Slice tuna into strips, $^1/_2$-inch thick and serve with chutney.

✳ Chutney can be stored in an airtight container in refrigerator for up to 2 weeks. Tuna can be stored in an airtight container in refrigerator for up to 2 days, but is best served fresh.

¤ *Tuna with Pepper Chutney*

FISH & VEGETABLES IN RED CURRY

SERVES 4

Add some cooked rice and your meal is complete with superb aroma, color and flavor.

INGREDIENTS

1 pound red snapper or sea bass,
  cut into 1-inch cubes
3 tablespoons canola oil
1 small onion, halved and thinly sliced
2 large garlic cloves, thinly sliced
2 teaspoons red curry paste
1½ cups chicken stock
1 cup coconut milk
1 small sweet potato, cut into
  1-inch cubes

1 cup shelled fresh green peas
6 oz. cherry tomatoes
1 tablespoon fish sauce

For serving:
2 tablespoons lemon juice
⅓ cup cilantro, coarsely chopped

PREPARATION

1. Remove fish from refrigerator about 20 minutes before cooking.

2. Heat a saucepan over medium heat, add canola oil, onion and garlic and sauté for about 5 minutes, stirring occasionally, until onion and garlic soften. Add curry paste and cook for 30 seconds, stirring continuously, until the curry aroma rises. Add chicken stock, coconut milk and sweet potato and bring to a boil.

3. Reduce heat and cook for 15 minutes, until the sweet potato is tender. Add fish, peas, cherry tomatoes and fish sauce and bring to a boil. Reduce heat, cover and cook for 5 minutes, until the fish is cooked.

4. Add lemon juice, sprinkle with cilantro and serve.

* This curry can be stored in an airtight container in refrigerator for up to 2 days. Reheat in microwave.

FISH
WITH
BROCCOLINI

SERVES 4

Light and super healthy, this stir-fry combines Asian flavors with nutrient-rich, low-calorie fish and broccolini.

INGREDIENTS

1¼ pounds red snapper or sea bass, cut into 2-inch cubes
1 pound broccolini, cut into 2-inch pieces
2 tablespoons canola oil
1 large garlic clove, coarsely chopped
1 tablespoon fresh ginger, thinly sliced
8 green onions, cut into 2-inch pieces
2 tablespoons fish sauce
2 tablespoons lemon juice
1 teaspoon sugar
Salt and ground black pepper, to taste

PREPARATION

1. Remove fish from refrigerator about 20 minutes before cooking.

2. Cook broccolini for 2 minutes in salted boiling water, until crisp-tender. Drain.

3. Heat wok over high heat, add canola oil, garlic and ginger and stir-fry for a minute, until aroma rises from the wok. Add fish and stir-fry for 3 minutes, until golden.

4. Add broccolini, green onion, fish sauce, lemon juice, sugar, salt and pepper and stir-fry for another minute, just until flavors are incorporated. Taste and adjust seasoning with salt and pepper.

✱ This fish dish can be stored in an airtight container in refrigerator for up to 2 days. Reheat in microwave.

MOROCCAN FISH TAGINE

SERVES 4

Cubes of fish are cooked quickly in this rich sauce.

INGREDIENTS

2 tablespoons olive oil

1 medium onion, coarsely chopped

1 medium yellow pepper, cut into
$1/2$-inch cubes

2 garlic cloves, coarsely chopped

3 medium tomatoes, cut into
$1/2$-inch cubes

1 teaspoon cumin

1 teaspoon sugar

$1/2$ teaspoon paprika

$1/2$ teaspoon ground coriander

2 cups water

Salt and ground black pepper, to taste

$1 1/4$ pounds red snapper or sea bass,
cut into 1-inch cubes

For serving:

$1/4$ cup cilantro or parsley, coarsely
chopped

PREPARATION

1. Remove fish from refrigerator about 20 minutes before cooking.

2. Heat a medium saucepan over medium heat, add olive oil, onion and pepper and sauté until tender.

3. Add garlic, tomatoes, cumin, sugar, paprika and coriander and sauté for 5 minutes, stirring continuously, until the tomatoes are tender. Add water, salt and pepper and bring to a boil. Taste and adjust seasoning with salt and pepper.

4. Add fish and bring to a boil again. Reduce heat, cover and cook for 5-8 minutes, until the fish is cooked.

5. Sprinkle with cilantro or parsley and serve.

* This tagine can be stored in an airtight container in refrigerator for up to 2 days. Reheat in microwave.

¤ Moroccan Fish Tagine

SALMON IN MUSTARD WITH FENNEL & OLIVES

SERVES 4

If fennel isn't your favorite, it can be substituted with 18 oz. of cherry tomatoes.

INGREDIENTS

4 fresh salmon fillets, skin-on, about 6 oz. each
2 tablespoons coarse grain Dijon mustard
2 fennel bulbs, cut into 1-inch cubes
16 Kalamata olives, pitted and halved
2 tablespoons olive oil
Salt and ground black pepper, to taste

PREPARATION

1. Remove fish from refrigerator at least 30 minutes before cooking.

2. Preheat oven to 400°F and line a baking pan with parchment paper. Place salmon in baking pan, skin side down and coat in Dijon mustard.

3. In a bowl, mix fennel, olives, olive oil, salt and pepper and place in baking pan around fish.

4. Bake for 20 minutes, until the fish is cooked.

✱ This fish dish can be stored in an airtight container in refrigerator for up to 2 days. Reheat in microwave.

SEA BREAM EN PAPILLOTE WITH PORTOBELLO MUSHROOMS

SERVES 4

En papillote *means 'in paper'. Fish is wrapped up in parchment paper and is baked in its own juices, resulting in a succulent, flavor-packed dish.*

INGREDIENTS

4 sea bream fillets with skin-on, about 7 oz. each
Salt and ground black pepper, to taste
1 tablespoon canola oil
2 tablespoons soy sauce
2 tablespoons dry white wine
3 tablespoons lemon juice
4 medium portobello mushrooms, cut into $1/4$-inch thick strips

PREPARATION

1. Remove fish from refrigerator about 20 minutes before cooking.

2. Preheat oven to 400°F. Prepare 4 sheets of parchment paper, place a sea bream fillet on each one, skin side down, and season with salt and pepper.

3. In a bowl, mix oil, soy sauce, wine and lemon juice. Pour 2 tablespoons of the sauce on each fillet, sprinkle with slices of mushroom and fold up the paper to create a sealed packet.

4. Bake for 10-12 minutes, until the fish is cooked.

✱ The fish can be stored in an airtight container in refrigerator for up to 2 days. Reheat in microwave.

GRILLED SALMON WITH AVOCADO & ORANGE SALSA

SERVES 4

Hot and cold go together:
oven-grilled salmon with a chilly
avocado and orange salsa.

INGREDIENTS

4 salmon fillets, skin-on, about 6 oz. each
2 tablespoons olive oil

For the salsa:
1 medium avocado, peeled and cut into $1/4$-inch cubes
1 medium orange, peeled and cut into $1/4$-inch cubes
2 tablespoons cilantro, finely chopped
1 garlic clove, crushed
1 teaspoon balsamic vinegar
Salt and ground black pepper, to taste

PREPARATION

1. Remove fish from refrigerator about 20 minutes before cooking.

2. Prepare the salsa: Mix all the salsa ingredients in a bowl. Taste and adjust seasoning with salt and pepper. Chill until ready to serve.

3. Prepare the fish: Preheat oven to 350°F and line a baking pan with parchment paper. Spread olive oil on the salmon and place in baking pan skin side down.

4. Bake for 15-20 minutes, until the fish is cooked.

5. Serve hot salmon with cold salsa.

* Store salsa and fish in refrigerator separately, each in an airtight container, for up to 2 days. Reheat salmon in microwave.

¤ *Grilled Salmon with Avocado & Orange Salsa*

CEVICHE

SERVES 4

A classic ceviche with tomatoes, fresh herbs and chili peppers.

INGREDIENTS

3/4 pound fresh white fish (grouper, mackerel, etc.),
   cut into 1/2-inch cubes (see Note below)
1 large tomato, cut into 1/2-inch cubes
2 tablespoons chives, finely chopped
2 tablespoons cilantro, finely chopped
1/2 hot chili pepper, thinly sliced
3 tablespoons lemon juice
2 tablespoons olive oil
Salt and ground black pepper, to taste

PREPARATION

Mix all ingredients in a bowl, taste and adjust seasoning with salt and pepper. Serve immediately.

Note: Eating raw fish carries a risk of foodborne illness. To avoid this risk, cook fish before marinating.

CEVICHE WITH BEETS

SERVES 4

The beets add brilliant color, essential nutrients and an earthy flavor to the ceviche.

INGREDIENTS

3/4 pound fresh white fish (grouper, mackerel, etc.),
   cut into 1/2-inch cubes (see Note below)
1 medium beet, cooked, peeled and cut into 1/2-inch cubes
1 shallot, finely chopped
2 tablespoons cilantro, finely chopped
1/4 cup lemon juice
2 tablespoons tahini
Salt and ground black pepper, to taste

PREPARATION

Mix all ingredients in a bowl, taste and adjust seasoning with salt and pepper. Serve immediately.

Note: Eating raw fish carries a risk of foodborne illness. To avoid this risk, cook fish before marinating.

SALMON & CHERRY TOMATO SKEWERS IN TERIYAKI SAUCE

MAKES 20 SKEWERS

Keep the baking time for the salmon down to a minimum, so as not to dry it out.

INGREDIENTS

1^1/$_4$ pounds fresh skinless salmon fillet, cut into 1^1/$_2$-inch cubes
40 cherry tomatoes (2 colors are recommended)

For the teriyaki sauce:
^{1}/$_4$ cup mirin
^{1}/$_4$ cup soy sauce
2 tablespoons sake or dry white wine
1 tablespoon dark brown sugar
1 tablespoon canola oil
1 teaspoon sesame oil
2 teaspoons ginger, finely grated

PREPARATION

1. Mix sauce ingredients in a bowl, until sugar is dissolved. Add cubes of fish and stir well. Marinate for 30 minutes at room temperature.

2. Preheat oven to 350°F and line a baking sheet with parchment paper. Alternately place 2 cubes of salmon and 2 cherry tomatoes on each skewer and place on baking sheet.

3. Bake for 8-10 minutes, just until the fish is cooked.

✳ The skewers can be stored in an airtight container in refrigerator for up to 2 days. Reheat in microwave.

¤ *Salmon & Cherry Tomato Skewers in Teriyaki Sauce*

INDEX

CONVERSION CHARTS

Standard United States measures are used for the recipes in this cookbook. The information presented in the following Conversion Charts can be used to determine *approximate* metric equivalents.

METRIC EQUIVALENTS
FOR DIFFERENT TYPES OF INGREDIENTS

A standard cup measure of a dry or solid ingredient will vary in weight depending on the type of ingredient. A standard cup of liquid is the same volume for any type of liquid. Use the following chart when converting standard cup measures to grams (weight) or milliliters (volume).

Standard Cup		Fine Powder (ex. flour)		Grain (ex.rice)		Granular (ex. sugar)		Liquid Solids (ex. butter)		Liquid (ex. milk)
1	=	140 g	=	150 g	=	190 g	=	200 g	=	240 ml
3/4	=	105 g	=	113 g	=	143 g	=	150 g	=	180 ml
2/3	=	93 g	=	100 g	=	125 g	=	133 g	=	160 ml
1/2	=	70 g	=	75 g	=	95 g	=	100 g	=	120 ml
1/3	=	47 g	=	50 g	=	63 g	=	67 g	=	80 ml
1/4	=	35 g	=	38 g	=	48 g	=	50 g	=	60 ml
1/8	=	18 g	=	19 g	=	24 g	=	25 g	=	30 ml

USEFUL EQUIVALENTS FOR DRY INGREDIENTS BY WEIGHT

To convert ounces to grams, multiply the number of oz by 30

1 oz	=	$^1/_{16}$ lb	=	30 g
4 oz	=	$^1/_4$ lb	=	120 g
8 oz	=	$^1/_2$ lb	=	240 g
12 oz	=	$^3/_4$ lb	–	360 g
16 oz	=	1 lb	=	480 g

USEFUL EQUIVALENTS FOR LENGTH

To convert inches to centimeters, multiply number of inches by 2.5

1 in				=	2.5 cm		
6 in	=	$^1/_2$ ft		=	15 cm		
12 in	=	1 ft		=	30 cm		
36 in	=	3 ft	=	1 yd	=	90 cm		
40 in				=	100 cm	=	1 m

USEFUL EQUIVALENTS FOR COOKING/OVEN TEMPERATURES

	Fahrenheit		Celsius		Gas Mark
Freeze Water	32° F	=	0° C		
Room temperature	68° F	=	20° C		
Boil Water	212° F	=	100° C		
Bake	325° F	=	160° C	=	3
	350° F	=	180° C	=	4
	375° F	=	190° C	=	5
	400° F	=	200° C	=	6
	425° F	=	220° C	=	7
	450° F	=	230° C	=	8
Broil				=	Grill

USEFUL EQUIVALENTS FOR LIQUID INGREDIENTS BY VOLUME

$^1/_4$ tsp					=	1 ml
$^1/_2$ tsp					=	2 ml
1 tsp					=	5 ml
3 tsp	=	1 tbls		=	$^1/_2$ fl oz	=	15 ml
		2 tbls	=	$^1/_8$ cup	=	1 fl oz	=	30 ml
		4 tbls	=	$^1/_4$ cup	=	2 fl oz	=	60 ml
		$5^1/_3$ tbls	=	$^1/_3$ cup	=	3 fl oz	=	80 ml
		8 tbls	=	$^1/_2$ cup	=	4 fl oz	=	120 ml
		$10^2/_3$ tbls	=	$^2/_3$ cup	=	5 fl oz	–	160 ml
		12 tbls	=	$^3/_4$ cup	=	6 fl oz	=	180 ml
		16 tbls	=	1 cup	=	8 fl oz	=	240 ml
		1 pt	=	2 cups	=	16 fl oz	=	480 ml
		1 qt	=	4 cups	=	32 fl oz	=	960 ml
					33 fl oz	=	1000 ml (1 liter)

NOTES